Quick & Easy Scrap Quilting
in Mix and Match Sets

Edited by Jeanne Stauffer and Sandra L. Hatch

HOUSE of
WHITE
BIRCHES

Quick & Easy Scrap Quilting in Mix and Match Sets

Copyright © 2000 House of White Birches, Berne, Indiana 46711

Editors: Jeanne Stauffer, Sandra L. Hatch
Design Manager: Vicki Blizzard
Project Supervisor: Barb Sprunger
Technical Editor: Connie Rand
Copy Editors: Mary Nowak, Sue Harvey, Nicki Lehman
Publications Coordinator: Tanya Turner

Photography: Tammy Christian, Jeff Chilcote, Jennifer Fourman
Photography Stylist: Arlou Wittwer
Photography Assistant: Linda Quinlan

Production Coordinator: Brenda Gallmeyer
Book Design/Production: Vicki's Design Studio
Production Supervisor: Ronda Bechinski
Production Assistants: Shirley Blalock, Marj Morgan
Traffic Coordinator: Sandra Beres

Publishers: Carl H. Muselman, Arthur K. Muselman
Chief Executive Officer: John Robinson
Marketing Director: Scott Moss
Book Marketing Manager: Craig Scott
Product Development Director: Vivian Rothe
Publishing Services Manager: Brenda R. Wendling

Printed in the United States of America
First Printing: 2000
Library of Congress Number: 99-85881
ISBN: 1-882138-59-7

A note *from the* Editors

Dear Quilter,

Gather up your scraps and get ready for a good time! It was such a joy to select the designs for this book! We know you are going to find many projects that you will enjoy stitching.

Knowing that you have many fabric scraps in different sizes and colors, we have chosen a wide variety of patterns for you. Each one is guaranteed to provide you with hours of quilting enjoyment, from the time you gather your scraps and select your fabrics (and maybe go to your quilting shop to purchase even more!) to the time you put the last stitch in your binding.

You'll find a good mix of large and small quilts, designs using piecing, appliqué or both, and projects for the beginner and the experienced quilter. Some use only a few fabrics, and others use more than a hundred.

You'll start having fun creating fabulous quilts and quilted projects as soon as you open this book. You'll find instructions that are easy to understand and dozens of full-color drawings and photographs to help you along the way. We used the blocks of one pattern to create a second or even third matching design and give you many options.

To keep with our mix and match theme, we've selected vests with matching purses, table toppers with matching coasters, a denim exercise mat and gym bag duo, a pair of twin-bed quilts, matching denim dorm throw and doggie buddy, a coordinating denim outfit and purse, matching baby quilt and stuffed clown, and much more.

What a delight it has been to put this book together for you! We've managed to squeeze in over 65 scrappy, creative projects, all for your enjoyment. All of us who worked together to bring you this book wish you many relaxing and rewarding hours.

Happy quilting,

Jeanne Stauffer

Sandra L. Hatch

Contents

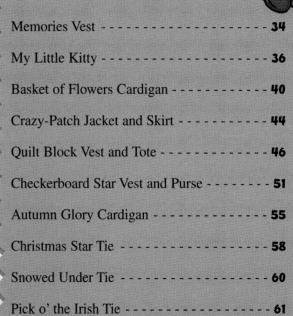

Chapter 3
Quilting All Around

Chapter 4
Delightful Denim Duos

Chapter 5
Quilts and More

Chapter 6
Quiltmaking Basics

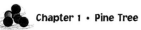

Pine Tree pattern begins on page 8.

Chapter 1
The Old and the New

No matter whether a scrap quilt is antique or newly completed, it has a story to tell. In this chapter, you'll find a story about each quilt and two methods, traditional and quick, for making them. Choose your favorite quilting method and have fun creating your own version of these scrappy quilts.

In This Chapter

Pine Tree

By Mary Jo Kurten

The Pine Tree is among the oldest traditional quilt patterns in our country. It honored our forefathers' Pine Tree flag, which centered a pine tree over the words "An Appeal to Heaven."

Pine Tree
11" x 11" Block

Pine Tree
Placement Diagram
62" x 77 1/2"

Project Notes

Although the Pine Tree block seems anything but easy, it can be made using quick-cutting methods even as a scrap quilt. Choose either the template method or the quicker method or a combination of both to complete your version of this lovely old quilt.

Each Pine Tree block is made using a primary fabric and a secondary fabric with white solid. In most blocks a print was used for the primary fabric with a coordinating solid. Our instructions are written for this combination.

Project Specifications

Skill Level: Intermediate

Quilt Size: 62" x 77 1/2"

Block Size: 11" x 11"

Number of Blocks: 12 plain and 20 pieced

Materials

- 5 1/4 yards white solid
- 20 rectangles 9" x 11" assorted prints or 1 1/2 yards
- 20 rectangles 6" x 10" coordinating solids or 1 yard
- Backing 66" x 82"
- Batting 66" x 82"
- 8 1/4 yards self-made or purchased binding
- White all-purpose thread
- 2 spools white quilting thread
- Basic sewing supplies and tools and rotary-cutting tools

Traditional Method

Step 1. Prepare templates using full-size patterns given; cut as directed on each piece for one block. Repeat for 20 blocks.

Step 2. To piece one block, sew print A triangles to white solid A triangles. Join six same-fabric A units to make a row as shown in Figure 1; sew a print A triangle to one end again referring to Figure 1. Repeat to make four rows. Repeat using coordinating solid and white solid A triangles.

Make 2

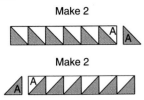

Make 2

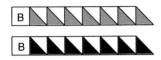

Figure 1
Join A units to make a row; sew
a print A to 1 end as shown.

Step 3. Sew a B square to one end of two rows of each fabric referring to Figure 2.

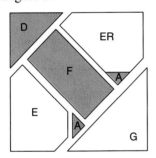

Figure 2
Sew B to 1 end of a pieced row.

Step 4. Sew print A to E and ER; sew to F. Add D and G as shown in Figure 3.

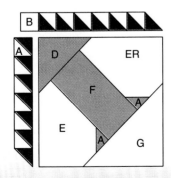

Figure 3
Join pieces as shown.

Step 5. Sew a pieced coordinating-solid A row to the pieced unit as shown in Figure 4; add an A-B row, again referring to Figure 4. Continue adding A rows and B rows, alternating print-A rows with coordinating-solid A rows.

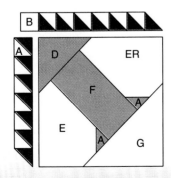

Figure 4
Sew an A row to the pieced unit;
add a B row as shown.

Step 6. Sew C to each side of the pieced unit to complete one block as shown in Figure 5. Repeat for 20 blocks.

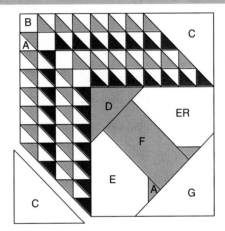

Figure 5
Sew C to pieced unit to complete 1 block.

Step 7. Cut the following from white solid: 12 squares 11 1/2" x 11 1/2" for H squares; four squares 16 7/8" x 16 7/8"—cut on both diagonals to make 16 I triangles (discard two); two squares 8 3/4" x 8 3/4"—cut in half on one diagonal to make J triangles.

Step 8. Arrange pieced blocks with H, I and J in diagonal rows as shown in Figure 6. Join in rows; join rows to complete pieced center.

Figure 6
Arrange pieced blocks with H, I
and J in diagonal rows.

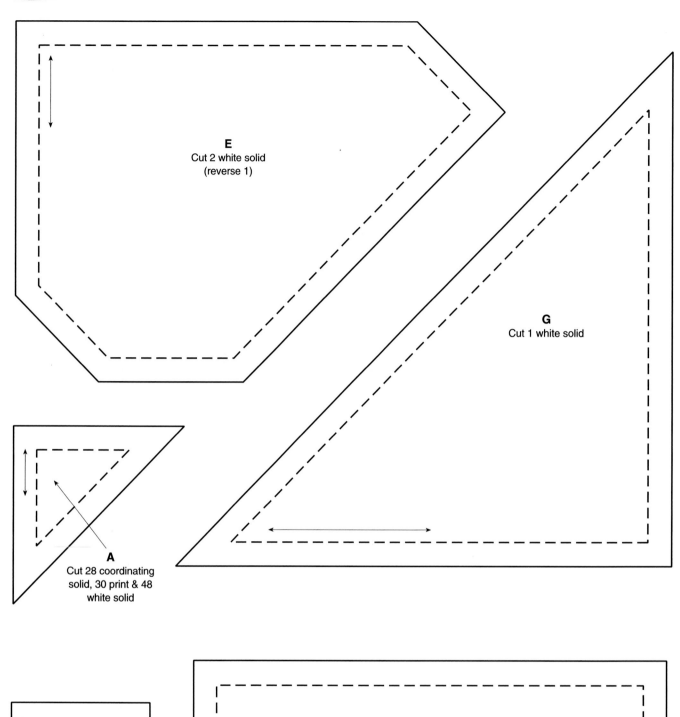

E
Cut 2 white solid
(reverse 1)

G
Cut 1 white solid

A
Cut 28 coordinating
solid, 30 print & 48
white solid

B
Cut 4 white solid

F
Cut 1 print

Step 9. Prepare top for quilting and finish as desired referring to the General Instructions. *Note: The quilt shown was quilted in a diagonal 1" grid throughout.*

Quick Method

Step 1. Cut the following from white solid: three strips 4 7/8" by fabric width—subcut into twenty 4 7/8" squares and cut in half on one diagonal for C triangles; and two strips 5 3/8" by fabric width—subcut into ten 5 3/8" squares and cut in half on one diagonal for G triangles.

Step 2. Prepare template for E using pattern given. Cut five strips white solid 3 3/4" by fabric width. Place E on strip as shown in Figure 7; trace and cut 20 E pieces. Reverse E; place on strip and trace and cut 20 ER pieces.

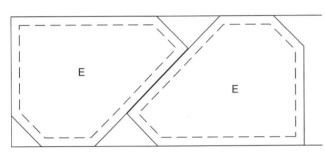

Figure 7
Place E on strip as shown.

Step 3. Cut three strips white solid 1 1/2" by fabric width; subcut into eighty 1 1/2" segments for B.

Step 4. Cut 22 strips white solid 1 7/8" by fabric width; subcut into 1 7/8" segments. You will need 480 segments. Cut each segment in half on one diagonal to make a triangle; you will need 960 A triangles.

Step 5. Prepare templates for D and F pieces

using patterns given. From each 9" x 11" print rectangle, cut one each D and F as shown in Figure 8. From the remainder, cut four 1 7/8"-wide strips, again referring to Figure 8. Subcut into fifteen 1 7/8" units; cut each unit in half on one diagonal for A triangles.

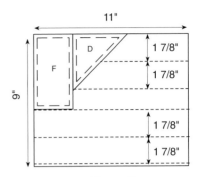

Figure 8
Cut D and F from print rectangle; cut remainder into 1 7/8"-wide strips as shown.

Step 6. From each 6" x 10" coordinating solid rectangle, cut three strips 1 7/8" x 10"; subcut into fourteen 1 7/8" units. Cut each unit in half on one diagonal for A triangles.

Step 7. Piece blocks and finish quilt as for Traditional Method Steps 2–9. ◢

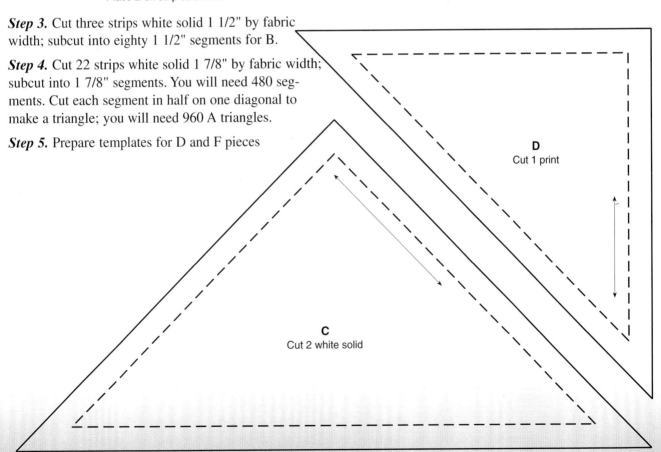

D
Cut 1 print

C
Cut 2 white solid

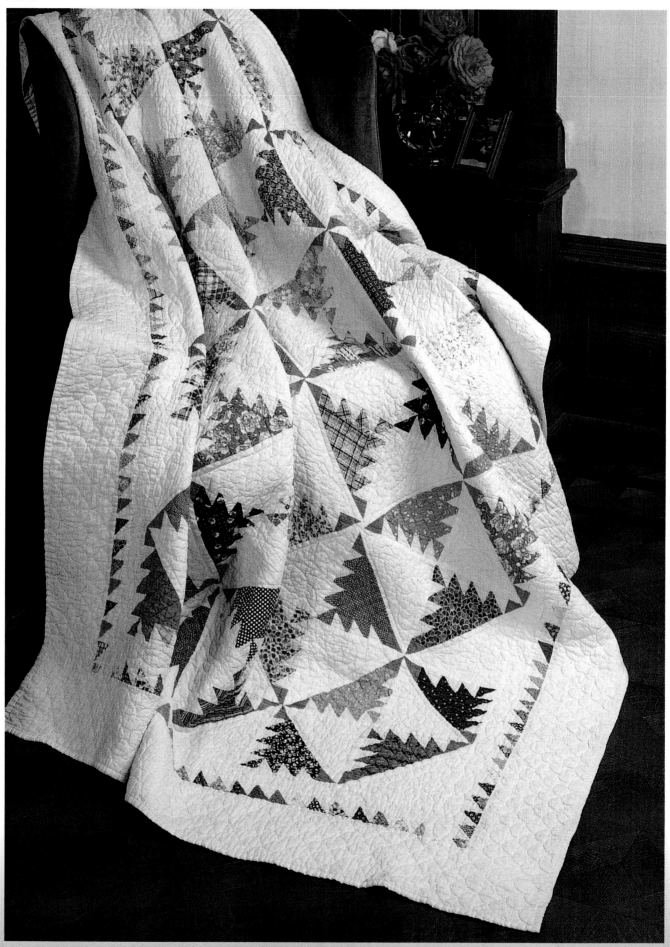

Delectable Mountains Variation

By Barb Sprunger

One of the charms of an antique quilt is that somehow the quilt goes together and comes out square. We strive for perfection; although it may not be stitched together accurately, the results can be beautiful, even when things are not always perfect.

Delectable Mountains Variation
Placement Diagram
77" x 84 1/2"

Delectable Mountains Variation
7 1/2" x 7 1/2" Block

Project Specifications

Skill Level: Intermediate

Quilt Size: 77" x 84 1/2"

Block Size: 7 1/2" x 7 1/2"

Number of Blocks: 72

Materials

- 72 rectangles assorted prints 8" x 10" or 2 3/4 yards total print scraps
- 1/2 yard peach solid
- 4 1/2 yards white solid
- Backing 81" x 89"
- Batting 81" x 89"
- 9 1/2 yards self-made or purchased binding
- All-purpose thread to match fabrics
- White quilting thread
- Basic sewing supplies and tools and rotary-cutting tools

Traditional Method

Step 1. Prepare templates using full-size patterns given; cut as directed on each piece for one block. Repeat for 72 blocks. *Note: If using 8" x 10" rectangles for prints, cut border triangles from portions left after cutting blocks.*

Step 2. To piece one block, sew a print A to a white solid A; repeat for seven A-A units.

Step 3. Join three A-A units to make a strip; repeat with four A-A units to make another strip referring to Figure 1.

Step 4. Sew a peach solid A triangle to one end of each strip as shown in Figure 2.

Figure 1
Join A-A units to make strips as shown.

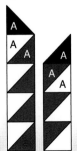

Figure 2
Sew a peach solid A to 1 end of each strip as shown.

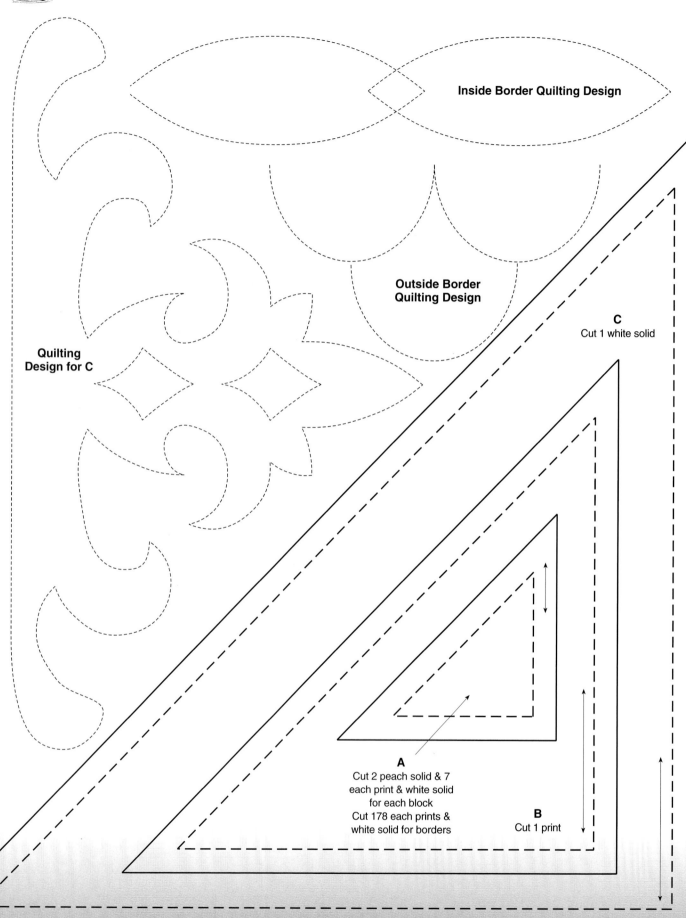

Inside Border Quilting Design

Outside Border
Quilting Design

Quilting
Design for C

C
Cut 1 white solid

A
Cut 2 peach solid & 7
each print & white solid
for each block
Cut 178 each prints &
white solid for borders

B
Cut 1 print

Step 5. Sew the three-unit strip to one short side of B and add the four-unit strip to the other short side of B as shown in Figure 3.

Step 6. Add C to the pieced unit to complete one block as shown in Figure 4; press. Repeat for 72 blocks.

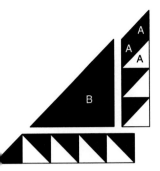
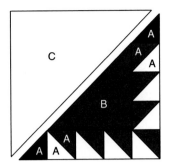

Figure 3
Sew the A strips to B as shown.

Figure 4
Add C to the pieced unit to complete 1 block.

Step 7. Join eight blocks to make a row as shown in Figure 5; repeat for nine rows. Press seams in one direction. Join pieced rows referring to the Placement Diagram to complete pieced center.

Figure 5
Join 8 blocks to make a row as shown.

Step 8. Cut and piece two strips white solid 2" x 60 1/2". Sew a strip to the top and bottom of the pieced center; press seams toward strips.

Step 9. Cut A pieces as directed on template for borders. Join 40 A-A units to make a strip referring to the Placement Diagram; press. Repeat for two strips.

Step 10. Sew a pieced strip to the top and bottom of the pieced center; press seams toward white solid strips.

Step 11. Cut and piece two strips white solid 2" x 74". Sew a strip to opposite long sides of the pieced center; press seams toward strips.

Step 12. Join 49 A-A units to make a strip referring to the Placement Diagram; press. Repeat for two strips.

Step 13. Sew a pieced strip to opposite long sides of the pieced center; press seams toward white solid strips.

Step 14. Cut and piece two strips each white solid 6" x 66 1/2" and 6" x 85". Sew the shorter strips to the top and bottom and longer strips to opposite sides of the pieced center; press seams toward white solid strips.

Step 15. Mark the quilting designs given in C and on borders referring to General Instructions.

Step 16. Prepare top for quilting and finish as desired referring to the General Instructions.

Delectible Mountain Memories

I have fond memories as I think of my grandmother, Lydia Lehman, who made and quilted this Bear Paw quilt in the 1930s.

A native of northeastern Indiana, Lydia was born in 1893 and died shortly after her 100th birthday.

She used a variety of scraps from my aunt's and mother's dresses in this quilt. After the quilt top was hand pieced together and put in the frame, friends and family would often stop by to help with the quilting. My mother Lorraine remembers this being an especially fun time for her and her cousins, who would play while their mothers quilted. The children loved to hide uner the quilt frame and listen to grown-up conversations.

I'm sure Grandma was very proud of this quilt when it was all completed. It kept family members warm in bed many a cold, winter's night upstairs in the old farmhouse.

Quick Method

Step 1. Cut 8" x 10" print rectangles into one 5 3/8" x 5 3/8" square and 2 3/8" x 2 3/8" squares as shown in Figure 6.

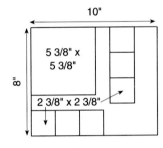

Figure 6
Cut 8" x 10" print rectangles as shown.

Step 2. Cut each 2 3/8" x 2 3/8" square in half on one diagonal to make A triangles. Select seven triangles of each print for blocks; set aside remainder for borders.

Step 3. Cut the 5 3/8" x 5 3/8" square in half on one diagonal to make B triangles. Set aside one triangle for another project.

Step 4. Cut peach solid into five strips 2 3/8" by fabric width. Subcut strip into 2 3/8" segments; you will need 72 segments. Cut each segment in half on one diagonal to make A triangles. You will need two peach solid A triangles for each block or 144 for whole quilt.

Step 5. Cut eight strips white solid 7 7/8" by fabric width. Subcut each strip into 7 7/8" segments. You will need 36 segments. Cut each segment in half on one diagonal to make 72 C triangles.

Step 6. Cut 21 strips white solid 2 3/8" by fabric width. Subcut each strip into 2 3/8" segments. Cut each segment in half on one diagonal to make A triangles. You will need seven white solid A triangles for each block and 178 for borders (total needed is 682).

Step 7. Join pieces to make blocks and complete quilt referring to Steps 2–16 of Traditional Method to finish.

Crazy-Patch Star

By Sandra L. Hatch

This beautiful, old pieced top gives a wonderful history of fabrics from the latter part of the 19th century. It is hand-stitched and hand-pieced.

Crazy-Patch Diamond
7" x 12" Unit

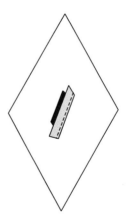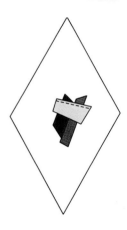

Crazy-Patch Star
Placement Diagram
72" x 77"

Project Specifications

Skill Level: Intermediate

Quilt Size: 72" x 77"

Unit Size: 7" x 12"

Number of Units: 24 half and 126 whole units

Materials

- 5 3/4 yards foundation fabric
- Assorted scraps red, dark and light fabrics
- Backing 76" x 81"
- Batting 76" x 81" (optional)
- 8 3/4 yards self-made or purchased binding
- All-purpose thread to match fabrics
- Basic sewing supplies and tools

Instructions

Step 1. Prepare template for diamond and half-diamond foundation using full-size pattern given; cut as directed.

Step 2. Select assorted red scraps. Place one scrap on the center of a diamond foundation piece with right side up. Place a second scrap to cover the first with right sides together; stitch across one side using a 1/4" seam allowance as shown in Figure 1.

Step 3. Finger-press the top piece right side up. Add another scrap along one side of the stitched area as shown in Figure 2. Trim seam allowance to 1/4", if

Figure 1
Place a second scrap to cover the first with right sides together; stitch across 1 side using a 1/4" seam allowance as shown.

Figure 2
Add another scrap along 1 side of the stitched area as shown.

necessary. Continue to add pieces until entire diamond foundation is covered.

Step 4. Trim excess fabrics even with diamond foundation as shown in Figure 3. Complete six red, 60 dark

Figure 3
Trim excess fabrics even with diamond foundation as shown.

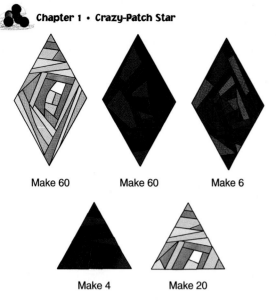

Make 60   Make 60   Make 6

Make 4   Make 20

Figure 4
Make diamonds as shown.

Figure 5
Arrange and join units in
6 sections as shown.

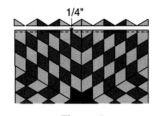

1/4"

Figure 6
Trim top and bottom edges 1/4" beyond
points of 4 full-diamond units as shown.

Crazy-Patch Star Memories

Several years ago our home was among those chosen for a Christmas tour in our community. During the tour I reacquainted myself with the real-estate agent who had sold us our camp over 18 years ago. Her mother was with her and they were very taken with my quilts and my work. Several weeks later the mother called me saying she had a quilt that I might be interested in. She brought it for me to look at and I bought it on the spot. I was taken by the crazy-patch diamonds and their tiny fabrics pieces.

When I hung this quilt to write the instructions, I discovered that the center star is out of kilter. What an interesting quilt. Who made it? Why is it hand-pieced and unfinished? Who cut it off like this to square it up? Why didn't they center that lovely red star? Too many questions.

I have decided to put a back on it with an opening so I can look at the back of the quilt if I want to. I won't square it up, but leave it as it is and hang it so others can discover its charm and start to wonder about its maker. It is definitely a conversation starter and may lead to many interesting theories.

A closer look at the individual star units shows some very creative curved piecing with very small pieces. Many blocks have this interesting feature. We also noticed that many blocks have a little red piece somewhere to tie it together with the red center star. This stitcher really enjoyed this type of piecing. It is unusual for a crazy quilt to have so many tiny hand-pieced scraps.

We have given instructions for the quilt with the star centered but if you would like a real conversation starter, maybe you'd like to work some magic of your own in the final layout.

and 60 light whole diamonds and four dark and 20 light half-diamond units as shown in Figure 4.

Step 5. Arrange and join units in six sections referring to Figure 5; press seams in one direction.

Step 6. Join sections to complete the pieced top; press seams in one direction.

Step 7. Trim top and bottom edges 1/4" beyond the points of four full-diamond units as shown in Figure 6.

Step 8. Prepare top for quilting or tying and finish as desired referring to the General Instructions. *Note: Many crazy-patch quilts are finished with no batting to reduce layers and eliminate quilting. It is difficult to hand-quilt through the fabric layers of a crazy-patch quilt so if batting is used, tying is recommended to hold layers together.* ◄

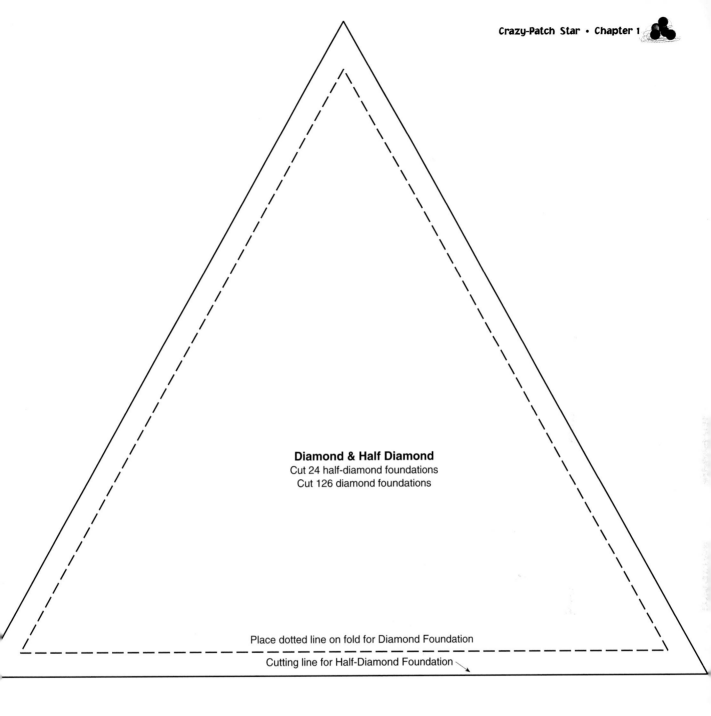

Diamond & Half Diamond
Cut 24 half-diamond foundations
Cut 126 diamond foundations

Place dotted line on fold for Diamond Foundation

Cutting line for Half-Diamond Foundation

Curved Crazy-Patch

Curved pieces were used in many of the old crazy quilts.
Most of those pieces were simply laid on the foundation
with other pieces and the edges were covered with fancy
embroidery stitches. In the quilt shown, the curved pieces
are actually stitched on in the same manner as the straight
pieces but with curved seams.

To accomplish this, lay a fabric patch on a pieced area;
pin in place. Draw a gentle curved line on the top piece
as shown in Figure 7; stitch along line. Trim excess
fabric; clip curve on top piece to smooth if necessary
as shown in Figure 8.

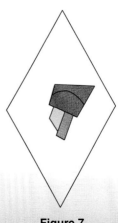

Figure 7
Draw a gentle curve
on the top piece.

Figure 8
Trim seam and clip curve.

Sunflower Star

By Mary Jo Kurten

A wide variety of pastels, shades of brown and shirting fabrics date this quilt as early as the 20th century. I was unsuccessful in my search for the pattern name, so I have given it a name based on the combination of two similar patterns.

Sunflower Star
9" x 9" Block

Sunflower Star
Placement Diagram
63 3/4" x 76 1/2"

Sunflower Star Memories

Among my favorite memories of Indiana are the Wednesday mornings my friend Emi and I set off at the crack of dawn for Shipshewana, drawn by the lure of an Amish auction. Quilts were No.1 on our acquisition priority list, and we couldn't wait for the first glimpse of what wonders might be hanging on the auction barn walls.

This quilt was one of several tops obviously pieced by one quilter, all during the same time period. I'm partial to circular patterns and was quick to claim this as my own. I've never been able to identify the pattern and would like to think it was the quilter's own design. Lydia Gerke brought the top to life with her wonderful quilting, and it remains one of my all-time favorites.

Project Note

There is really no quick way to piece the blocks in this lovely old quilt. The circular design surrounding the center star is best hand-pieced for accuracy. Adding the A and B pieces around the outside is also a difficult task and not for the beginner.

Project Specifications

Skill Level: Experienced
Quilt Size: 63 3/4" x 76 1/2"
Block Size: 9" x 9"
Number of Blocks: 20 plain and 30 pieced

Materials

- 3 1/2 yards white solid
- Wide variety of light, medium and dark brown and pastel scraps totaling 2 1/2 yards
- Backing 68" x 81"
- Batting 68" x 81"
- 8 1/4 yards self-made or purchased binding
- White all-purpose thread
- 2 spools white quilting thread
- Basic sewing supplies and tools

Instructions

Step 1. Prepare templates using full-size patterns given; cut as directed on each piece for one block. Repeat for 30 blocks.

Step 2. To piece one block, sew a dark print D to a medium print D, starting at the center dot and stopping at the 1/4" seam allowance as shown in Figure 1; repeat for four units. Join two units; repeat. Join these two units to complete pieced star as shown in Figure 2.

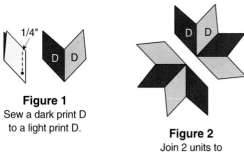

Figure 1
Sew a dark print D
to a light print D.

Figure 2
Join 2 units to
complete pieced star.

Step 3. Set C pieces into pieced star unit as shown in Figure 3.

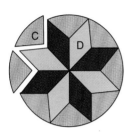

Figure 3
Set in C pieces as shown.

Step 4. Sew F to E; repeat for all F and E pieces. Join pieced units to make a circle; stitch to the C-D center star unit.

Step 5. Set in A and B pieces around the edges of the pieced unit referring to Figure 4 to finish one block; repeat for 30 blocks.

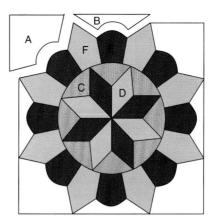

Figure 4
Set in A and B pieces as shown.

Step 6. Cut 20 squares white solid 9 1/2" x 9 1/2". Cut five squares white solid 14" x 14". Cut in half on both diagonals to make side fill-in triangles; discard two. Cut two squares white solid 7 1/4" x 7 1/4"; cut in half on one diagonal to make corner triangles.

Step 7. Lay out pieced blocks, plain blocks and side and corner triangles in diagonal rows as shown in Figure 5. Join blocks and triangles in rows; join rows to complete pieced center. Press seams in one direction.

9 1/2" x 9 1/2"

Figure 5
Arrange blocks and corner and
side triangles as shown.

Step 8. Mark the quilting design given on plain blocks referring to General Instructions.

Step 9. Prepare top for quilting and finish as desired referring to the General Instructions.

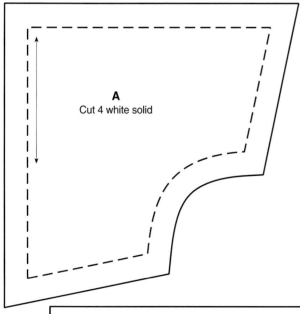

A
Cut 4 white solid

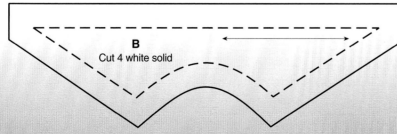

B
Cut 4 white solid

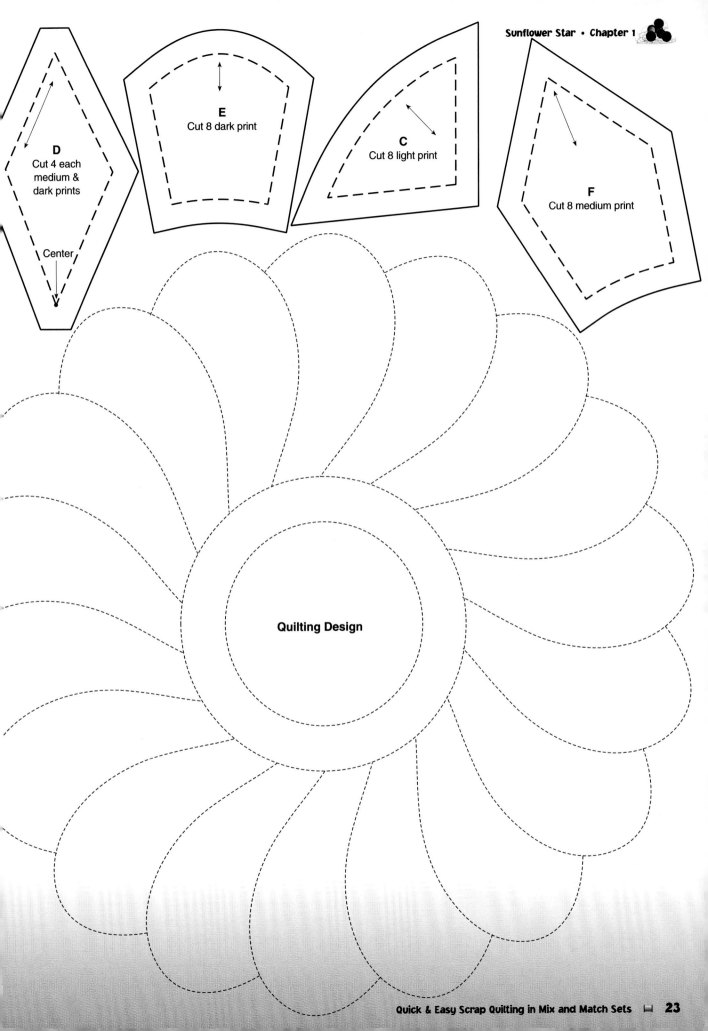

D
Cut 4 each
medium &
dark prints

Center

E
Cut 8 dark print

C
Cut 8 light print

F
Cut 8 medium print

Quilting Design

Multiple Irish Chain

By Jeanne Stauffer

Imagine using small squares for all the white areas in this quilt instead of one larger square—it makes you wonder why someone would do all that extra work.

Project Notes

To make this quilt using quicker methods, cut 2"-wide strips of a variety of fabrics. Use strips of varying length and butt them together when joining with other longer strips. This might mean sections of the strip may not be usable, but it will save lots of time. Look in your scrap basket and use leftover strips from other strip-pieced projects or other larger-size scraps cut into 2"-wide strips. If using up lots of scraps is your goal, this quilt is the perfect project for you.

Note that in the quick version we have made the large white areas from unpieced squares rather than pieced ones to save time and fabric.

Project Specifications

Skill Level: Intermediate

Quilt Size: 82 1/2" x 82 1/2"

Unit Size: 1 1/2" x 1 1/2"

Number of Units: 3025

Materials

- 1 1/2 yards green solid
- 2 1/4 yards white solid
- Assorted light and medium scrap prints
- Backing 87" x 87"
- Batting 87" x 87"
- 9 1/2 yards self-made or purchased binding
- All-purpose thread to match fabrics
- Basic sewing supplies and tools, rotary cutter, ruler and mat

Traditional Method

Step 1. Prepare template for square using full-size pattern given; cut as directed.

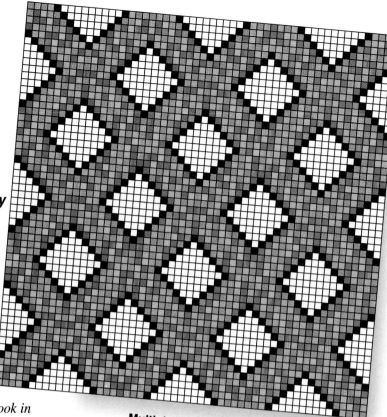

Multiple Irish Chain
Placement Diagram
82 1/2" x 82 1/2"

Step 2. Arrange squares to make units as shown in Figure 1. Join squares in rows; press seams in one direction. Join rows to complete units; press seams in one direction.

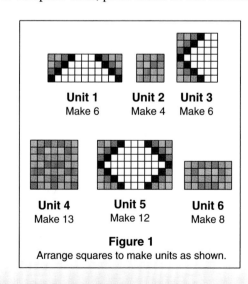

Unit 1
Make 6

Unit 2
Make 4

Unit 3
Make 6

Unit 4
Make 13

Unit 5
Make 12

Unit 6
Make 8

Figure 1
Arrange squares to make units as shown.

Step 3. Join remaining squares to make Row 1 as shown in Figure 2; repeat for six rows. Press seams in one direction.

Step 4. Join remaining units to make Row 2 as shown in Figure 3; repeat for six rows. Press seams in one direction.

Step 5. Join Row 1 with Row 2 to make Row 3 as shown in Figure 4; repeat for six rows.

Figure 2
Join remaining units to make Row 1 as shown.

Figure 3
Join remaining units to make Row 2 as shown.

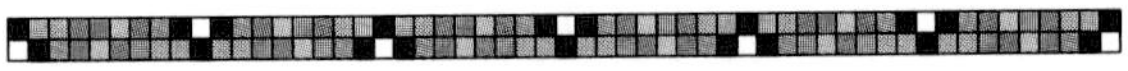

Figure 4
Join Row 1 with Row 2 to make Row 3 as shown.

Step 6. Lay out pieced units with Row 3 strips as shown in Figure 5. Join units to make rows; press seams in one direction. Join rows with strips to complete pieced top.

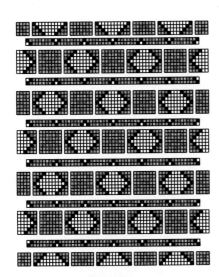

Figure 5
Lay out pieced units with Row 3 strips as shown.

Step 7. Prepare top for quilting and finish as desired referring to the General Instructions. *Note: The quilt shown was hand-quilted 1/4" inside every square.*

Quick Method

Step 1. Cut 21 strips green solid 2" by fabric width. *Note: If using scrap strips in Step 3, additional green solid strips may be needed.*

Step 2. Cut 16 strips white solid 2" by fabric width and four strips 8" by fabric width. Subcut 8"-wide strips into twelve 8" segments for E and twelve 5" segments for F. Subcut 2"-wide strips into thirty 5" segments for G and twelve 3 1/2" segments for H. Cut the remaining 2"-wide strips into 2" segments.

Step 3. Cut scrap prints into 2"-wide strips. *Note: If using 42"-wide strips, you will need 105 strips.*

However, scrap strips may vary in length from shorter strips to fabric-width strips. This does not matter. Strips are butted one 2"-edge to another to make longer strips as shown in Figure 6. Continue to cut scrap strips to make about 120 strips approximately 42" long to allow for unusable sections.

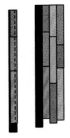

Figure 6
Join 3 scrap strips with a green solid strip, butting ends of scrap strip pieces as shown.

Step 4. Join three scrap strips with a green solid strip again referring to Figure 6. *Note: Scrap strips will refer to approximate 42"-long butted strips throughout the remainder of these instructions.* Repeat for four strip sets. Subcut strip sets into 2" segments to make 72 A units as shown in Figure 7. *Note: If many shorter scrap strips were used, additional sets may be needed to cut the required segments.*

Step 5. Join two scrap strips with a green solid strip; repeat for four strip sets. Subcut strip sets into 2" segments to make 72 B units as shown in Figure 8.

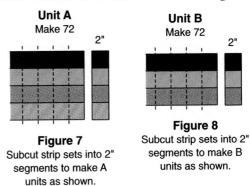

Unit A
Make 72

Unit B
Make 72

Figure 7
Subcut strip sets into 2" segments to make A units as shown.

Figure 8
Subcut strip sets into 2" segments to make B units as shown.

Step 6. Join one each scrap strip, green solid strip and white solid strip; repeat for four strip sets. Subcut strip sets into 2" segments to make 72 C units as shown in Figure 9.

Step 7. Join one green solid strip with two white solid strips; repeat for two strip sets. Subcut strip sets into 2" segments to make 42 D units as shown in Figure 10.

Step 8. Join four scrap strips; repeat for one strip set. Subcut strip set into 2" segments to make 16 I units as shown in Figure 11.

Step 9. Join seven scrap strips; repeat for 11 strip sets. Subcut strip sets into 2" segments to make 216 J units as shown in Figure 12.

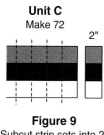

Unit C
Make 72

2"

Figure 9
Subcut strip sets into 2"
segments to make C
units as shown.

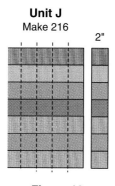

Unit D
Make 42

2"

Figure 10
Subcut strip sets into 2"
segments to make D
units as shown.

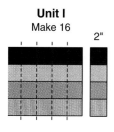

Unit I
Make 16

2"

Figure 11
Subcut strip sets into 2"
segments to make I
units as shown.

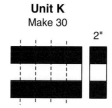

Unit J
Make 216

2"

Figure 12
Subcut strip sets into 2"
segments to make J
units as shown.

Step 10. Join two green solid strips with one white solid
strip; repeat for two strip sets. Subcut strip sets into 2" segments to make 30 K units as shown in Figure 13.

Unit K
Make 30

2"

Figure 13
Subcut strip sets into 2"
segments to make K
units as shown.

Step 11. Arrange pieced units with E squares and F, G and
H rectangles to make pieced units referring to Figure 14.

Step 12. Piece Rows 1 and 2 using pieced units with
white and green solid 2" segments referring to Figure 15.

Step 13. Complete quilt referring to Traditional
Methods Steps 5–7. ▄

Row 1
Make 6

J   K

Row 2
Make 6

J   K

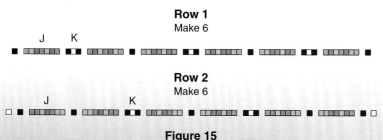

Figure 15
Piece Rows 1 and 2 using pieced units with white and green solid 2" segments.

Multiple Irish Chain Memories

I learned to quilt when my husband and I moved back
to his hometown. Many of the area churches still hold
quilting bees, and it was during one of these that I
discovered my husband's grandmother, Edna Stauffer,
was a quilter.

One day a woman mentioned that she had a quilt made
by Edna and wondered if I would like to have it. Of
course, my answer was yes.

When I took the quilt home, my husband remembered
seeing this quilt design on beds at his grandmother's
house many times. One of his aunts told me that this
design was a favorite of Edna's.

I look at all the tiny squares, 3025 of them, and wonder
how long it took to piece them together by hand.
Although I never met Edna, I share with her a love of
quilting and treasure the memory I have of her through
this beautifully hand-pieced quilt.

This quilt is now among my most treasured possessions.

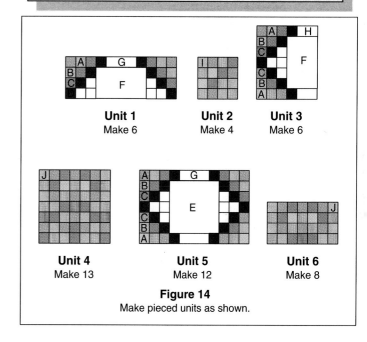

Unit 1
Make 6

Unit 2
Make 4

Unit 3
Make 6

Unit 4
Make 13

Unit 5
Make 12

Unit 6
Make 8

Figure 14
Make pieced units as shown.

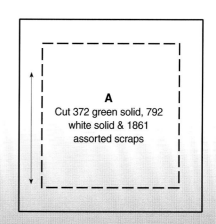

A
Cut 372 green solid, 792
white solid & 1861
assorted scraps

Kitty Corner

By Mary Jo Kurten

This old favorite also goes by the names Puss-in-the-Corner and Tic-Tac-Toe.

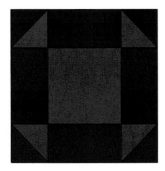

Kitty Corner
8" x 8" Block

Kitty Corner
Placement Diagram
72" x 80"

Project Specifications

Skill Level: Beginner

Quilt Size: 72" x 80"

Block Size: 8" x 8"

Number of Blocks: 45 plain and 45 pieced

Materials

- 1 1/4 yards total navy print scraps (6" x 8" piece of 45 print scraps for quick method)
- 2 1/8 yards total burgundy print scraps (8" x 11" piece of 45 print scraps for quick method)
- 2 1/4 yards navy solid for plain blocks
- Backing 76" x 84"
- Batting 76" x 84"
- 8 3/4 yards self-made or purchased binding
- All-purpose thread to match fabrics
- 2 spools navy quilting thread
- Basic sewing supplies and tools and rotary-cutting tools

Traditional Method

Step 1. Prepare templates using full-size patterns given; cut as directed on each piece for one block. Repeat for 45 blocks.

Step 2. To piece one block, sew a navy print B to a burgundy print B; repeat for four units. Arrange pieced units with A and C pieces and stitch together to complete one block as shown in Figure 1. Repeat for 45 blocks.

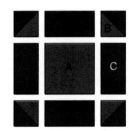

Figure 1
Arrange pieced units
with A and C as shown.

Step 3. Cut 45 squares navy solid 8 1/2" x 8 1/2".

Step 4. Join four pieced blocks with five navy solid blocks to make a row as shown in Figure 2; repeat for five rows. Press seams in one direction.

8 1/2" x
8 1/2"

Figure 2
Join 4 pieced blocks with 5 navy solid blocks to make a row.

Step 5. Join five pieced blocks with four navy solid blocks to make a row as shown in Figure 3; repeat for five rows. Press seams in one direction.

8 1/2" x
8 1/2"

Figure 3
Join 5 pieced blocks with 4 navy solid blocks to make a row.

Step 6. Join pieced rows referring to the Placement Diagram to complete the pieced top.

Step 7. Mark the quilting design given on plain blocks referring to General Instructions.

Step 8. Prepare top for quilting and finish as desired referring to the General Instructions.

Quick Method

Step 1. Cut each 6" x 8" piece navy print into two 2 7/8" x 2 7/8" squares for B and one 4 1/2" x 4 1/2" square for A.

Step 2. Cut each 8" x 11" piece burgundy print into four 2 1/2" x 4 1/2" rectangles for C and two 2 7/8" x 2 7/8" squares for B.

Step 3. Layer a navy print B with a burgundy print B with right sides together.

Step 4. Draw a line through the diagonal on the wrong side of one of the layered squares referring to Figure 4.

Figure 4
Mark the diagonal
on the wrong side
of 1 square in each
pair as shown.

Step 5. Sew together 1/4" away from each side of the diagonal line as shown in Figure 5. Cut apart on the diagonal line to make two right triangle squares as shown in Figure 6. Repeat to make four squares for each block.

Figure 5
Sew together 1/4" away
from each side of the
diagonal line as shown.

Step 6. Cut nine strips navy blue solid 8 1/2" by fabric width. Cut apart in 8 1/2" segments to make plain squares. You will need 45 plain squares.

Step 7. Piece blocks and complete quilt referring to Steps 4–8 of Traditional Method. ◣

Figure 6
Cut apart on the diagonal line to make
right triangle squares as shown.

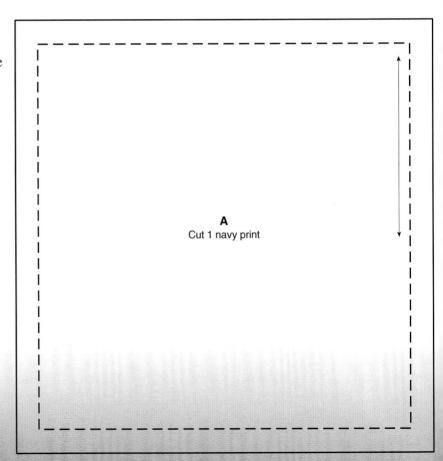

A
Cut 1 navy print

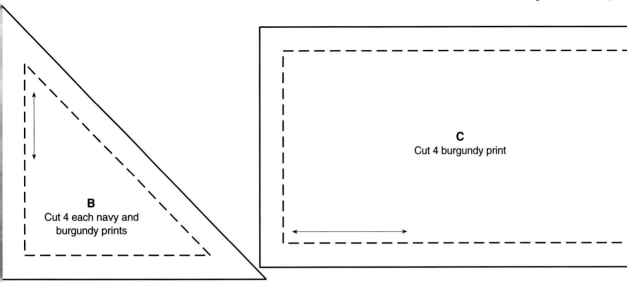

B
Cut 4 each navy and
burgundy prints

C
Cut 4 burgundy print

**Quilting
Design**

Memories Vest begins on page 34

Chapter 2
The Wearable Collection

Match your favorite quilting technique, piecing or appliqué, with a fun project in this chapter, and you'll have a good time both making and wearing these quilted garments while turning your stash of fabric into fashionable attire for the young and not-so-young.

In This Chapter

Memories Vest

By Beth Wheeler

Remember Dad with this vest made from his old ties. Make the vest for him, for you or for another family member as a very special tangible memory bank.

Memories
4" x 4" Block

Memories Vest
Placement Diagram
Size Varies

Project Notes

The sample vest was made using McCalls 5108 pattern, view A. If this pattern number has been discontinued, look for a vest pattern with a similar style. There is always a vest pattern available in this style, but the numbers do frequently change.

Ties come in a variety of widths, making it difficult for us to tell you how many ties you will need for one vest. Wider ties yield more squares; narrower ties may yield only one or two squares. Be sure you have enough ties to complete the vest before beginning construction.

Project Specifications

Skill Level: Beginner

Vest Size: Size varies

Block Size: 4" x 4"

Number of Blocks: Number varies with vest size

Materials

- Commercial vest pattern
- Approximately 20 old ties—half light and half dark
- Lining fabric according to pattern
- 3/4 yard lightweight fusible interfacing
- All-purpose thread to match fabrics
- 3 (5/8") buttons to match lining fabric
- Basic sewing supplies and tools and rotary cutter, ruler and mat

Instructions

Step 1. Clean ties, open seams and press open. *Note: The ties used on the sample were silk so they were dry-cleaned before using.*

Step 2. Bond fusible interfacing to the wrong side of wider part of ties following manufacturer's instructions.

Step 3. Cut 5 1/4" x 5 1/4" squares from each tie. You will need 17 each light and dark squares. Layer one dark and one light square with right sides together.

Step 4. Draw a diagonal line from corner to corner on the light square side of the layered units as shown in Figure 1. Stitch 1/4" away from the drawn line on each side. Cut along the drawn line to make two triangle/squares as shown in Figure 2.

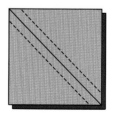

Figure 1
Draw a diagonal line on the light square side of the layered units; stitch 1/4" on each side of line.

Figure 2
Cut along the drawn line to make 2 triangle/squares as shown.

Step 5. Cut each triangle/square in half on the unstitched diagonal as shown in Figure 3; repeat for all units. Press seams in one direction.

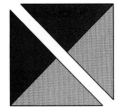

Figure 3
Cut each triangle/square in half
on the unstitched diagonal.

Step 6. Join two pieced units to create one block as shown in Figure 4; repeat for all units. **Note:** *Make 34 blocks for a size 42–44 vest; a larger vest may require additional squares.*

Figure 4
Join 2 pieced units to
create 1 block as shown.

Step 7. Arrange blocks in rows to create two panels as shown in Figure 5, making a left and right front. Join blocks in rows; join rows to complete a panel; press seams in one direction.

Figure 5
Arrange blocks in rows to
create 2 panels as shown.

Step 8. Place commercial vest front pattern face down on one panel; cut out. Place vest front pattern face up on remaining panel; cut out.

Step 9. Assemble vest and finish referring to pattern instructions.

Step 10. Make three buttonholes evenly spaced on left front. Sew buttons on right front to finish. ▣

My Little Kitty

By Michele Crawford

Stitch up a child's dressy jacket to coordinate with any outfit for a dressy but casual look.

My Little Kitty
Placement Diagram
Size Varies

Project Note

Purchase a T-shirt one size larger than an ordinary fit so it will fit over other clothes easily. Prewash knit shirt and fabrics before cutting. Handle shirt carefully to avoid stretching once the ribbing and center front have been cut away. Use a 1/4" seam allowance throughout. Press seams open to reduce bulk.

Project Specifications

Skill Level: Beginner

Jacket Size: Size varies

Materials

- Purchased cream long-sleeve knit T-shirt (girls 8–10)
- 1 strip each 3 different blue prints 1 1/2" x 25"
- 1 strip each 3 different pink prints 1 1/2" x 25"
- 1 strip cream/blue/pink print 1 1/2" x 25"
- 9" x 9" square blue plaid
- 6 1/2" x 8 1/2" tan print
- 1" x 3" white print
- 1/2" x 2 1/2" pink solid
- Variety of scraps for patches
- Pink, blue and medium brown all-purpose thread
- 1/4 yard fusible transfer web
- 1/4 yard tear-off fabric stabilizer
- 1 package pink/white check single-fold bias tape
- 1 package pink wide bias tape
- 1 skein each white, black and pink embroidery floss
- 1 skein medium blue rayon floss
- 1/3 yard 1/8"-wide pink satin ribbon
- 2 small pink star buttons
- 2 (3/4") round wooden buttons
- Basic sewing supplies and tools, rotary cutter, ruler and cutting mat, pinking shears, water-erasable marker and tapestry needle

Instructions

Step 1. Cut off the bottom hem of the knit shirt. Determine how long the finished jacket will be with the pieced hem. Cut off the knit shirt, if necessary to make jacket finish at desired finished length. *Note: The pieced hem will add 2 1/4" to the length of the shirt. The hem was cut off and then an additional 4" was cut off above the original cut on the shirt shown.*

Step 2. Measure and cut down the center of the shirt front. Cut off the neckline ribbing. Place the shirt on the child. Use a pencil to draw a V-neck opening. Cut this opening on both sides of the shirt.

Step 3. For the pieced hem, measure around the raw edge of the shirt. *Note: The shirt used in the sample was 35 1/2". The directions will be for this shirt. Make any adjustments necessary when using a different size shirt by adding additional 1 1/2"-wide strips for a larger shirt or by removing strips for a smaller shirt.*

Step 4. Alternating colors and fabrics, sew the seven 1 1/2" x 25" strips with right sides together along length as shown in Figure 1. The stripped fabric will now measure 7 1/2" x 25". Cut five 4 1/2" segments from the stripped fabric again referring to Figure 1.

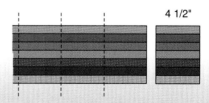

4 1/2"

Figure 1
Sew strips together in color order;
cut into 4 1/2" segments.

Step 5. Alternating colors, join the five segments to make a 35 1/2"-long strip for the hem as shown in Figure 2.

Figure 2
Alternating colors, join the 5 segments to
make a 35 1/2"-long strip for the hem.

Step 6. Pin the pieced hem evenly around the bottom of the shirt as shown in Figure 3; stitch. Press the seam toward the pieced section. Cut a 35 1/2" piece of pink/white check single-fold bias tape. Pin, then sew to the raw edge of the pieced hem; press seam toward pieced hem.

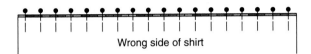

Wrong side of shirt

Figure 3
Pin the pieced hem evenly around the bottom of the shirt.

Step 7. Fold the pieced hem toward the inside of the jacket with pressed edge of bias tape covering the seam allowance of the pieced hem on the shirt as shown in Figure 4; pin. Hand-stitch the bias tape to the seam line.

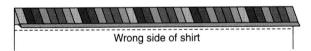

Wrong side of shirt

Figure 4
Fold the pieced hem toward the inside of the jacket with pressed edge of bias tape meeting the seam of the pieced hem on the shirt.

Step 8. Bind front edges and neckline using pink wide bias tape referring to the General Instructions.

Step 9. Use the tapestry needle and 6 strands of medium blue rayon floss to hand-sew a running stitch 1/4" from the wide bias tape, the pieced hem and the armhole seams.

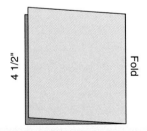

4 1/2"

Fold

Figure 5
Fold each strip in half as shown.

Step 10. Cut off each sleeve hem. Cut two 4 1/2" x 8 1/2" strips blue plaid. *Note: The bottom of the sleeve on the sample is 4" in diameter. Make any adjustments in the length of the fabric used for another size.* Fold

each strip in half as shown in Figure 5; pin and stitch along the short edge to make cuffs; press.

Step 11. Press one 8 1/2" raw edge of each cuff piece under 1/4". With right sides together, center the raw edge of each cuff to the raw edge of the bottom of the sleeve; pin and stitch. Press seam toward cuff piece. Fold cuffs in half with pressed edges of cuffs covering the seam allowance of the cuff edge already stitched to the sleeve as shown in Figure 6; pin and hand-stitch in place. Fold cuffs up on the sleeve front.

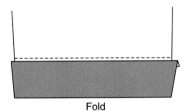

Fold

Figure 6
Fold cuffs in half with pressed
edges of cuffs meeting the seam of
the cuff and the sleeve as shown.

Step 12. Prepare templates for appliqué shapes using patterns given. Trace two cat shapes on paper side of fusible transfer web, reversing one. Repeat for leg, muzzle and ear pieces. Cut out shapes leaving a margin around each piece. Fuse to the wrong side of fabrics as directed on pattern pieces for color. Cut out shapes on traced lines; remove paper backing.

Step 13. Center a cat on each shirt front above the pieced hem with tail toward the side seam; fuse in place. Center and fuse a muzzle, two legs and two inside ear pieces on each cat. Draw eyes, nose and muzzle details in place with water-erasable marker.

Step 14. Cut two 5" x 7" pieces tear-off fabric stabilizer. Center a piece on the wrong side of the shirt behind each cat; pin in place. Using a machine buttonhole stitch, sew around cat shape and legs using medium brown all-purpose thread and around muzzle using pink all-purpose thread. Satin-stitch around each inside ear piece using pink all-purpose thread.

Step 15. Using 4 strands black embroidery floss, sew a French knot for each eye as marked on pattern for positioning. Use 2 strands white embroidery floss to sew a long stitch for each whisker. Use 2 strands pink embroidery floss to satin-stitch each nose.

Step 16. Tie two small bows with the 1/8"-wide pink satin ribbon. Sew a bow to the end of each tail. Sew a small pink star button to each cat's chest referring to the pattern for positioning.

Step 17. Bond fusible transfer web to blue and pink scraps. Using pinking shears, cut four blue and two pink patches of assorted sizes from scraps (2" square, 2 1/2" square and 2 1/2" x 3" rectangles used on sample). Remove paper backing; position and overlap two blue and one pink fused piece on each sweatshirt front above the cat referring to the project photo and Placement Diagram for positioning; fuse in place. Topstitch around each fused piece 1/8" from pinked edge using matching all-purpose thread.

Step 18. Sew a 3/4" round wooden button in the center of each group of patches to finish. ◨

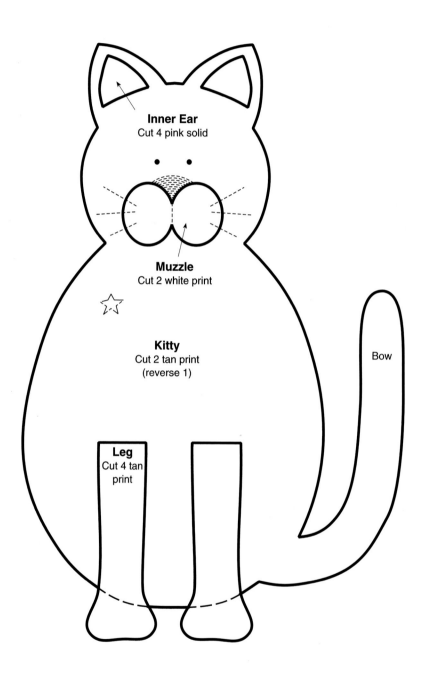

Inner Ear
Cut 4 pink solid

Muzzle
Cut 2 white print

Kitty
Cut 2 tan print
(reverse 1)

Leg
Cut 4 tan print

Bow

Basket of Flowers Cardigan

By Beth Wheeler

Turn a plain and simple white sweatshirt into an elegant cardigan with simple appliqué techniques.

Basket of Flowers Cardigan
Placement Diagram
Size Varies

Project Specifications

Skill Level: Beginner

Cardigan Size: Size varies

Materials

- White or light-colored sweatshirt with set-in or raglan sleeves
- Assorted light green and peach print scraps
- 18" square multicolored print
- 1/4 yard white-on-cream print
- White all-purpose thread
- Variegated beige, peach and green rayon thread
- 1/2 yard iron-on fabric stabilizer
- 1/2 yard fusible transfer web
- Craft glue (optional)
- Basic sewing supplies and tools

Instructions

Step 1. Cut sweatshirt down the center front. Cut off neck ribbing and hemline ribbing. Remove sleeve cuffs and cut sleeves to desired length. Round bottom and neck corners on front sides as shown in Figure 1.

Step 2. Prepare templates for appliqué shapes using pattern pieces given. Trace shapes onto the paper side of the fusible transfer web, leaving space between shapes and referring to the pattern pieces for number to cut. Cut out shapes, leaving a margin around each one.

Step 3. Fuse cut shapes to the wrong side of fabric scraps referring to the pattern pieces for color. Cut out shapes on traced lines; remove paper backing.

Step 4. Position basket shape in place on sweatshirt left

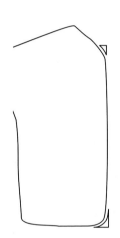

Figure 1
Round corners on sweatshirt fronts.

front referring to the Placement Diagram and photo of project for positioning suggestions; fuse in place.

Step 5. Iron a piece of iron-on fabric stabilizer behind basket shape. Stitch the cross-hatch pattern on the basket using variegated beige rayon thread in the top of the machine and white-all-purpose thread in the bobbin. Satin-stitch around the basket with the same thread; remove stabilizer.

Step 6. Cut three 3/4" x 18" strips white-on-cream print. Braid strips together for handle. Cut to desired length; glue or hand-stitch in place above basket.

Step 7. Arrange four flowers, four flower centers and five leaves on basket in numerical order referring to Figure 2 (see page 42), the Placement Diagram and the photo of project for positioning suggestions. Fuse shapes in place. Repeat with remaining pieces on the top right front of sweatshirt referring to Figure 3 (see page 42).

Step 8. Iron pieces of iron-on fabric stabilizer under each area to be appliquéd following manufacturer's instructions.

Step 9. Satin-stitch around each flower center with varie-gated-green rayon thread in the top of the machine and white all-purpose thread in the bobbin. Repeat down the center and around edges of each leaf with variegated-green

rayon thread and around each flower with variegated-peach rayon thread; remove the stabilizer.

Step 10. Prepare 3 yards bias binding using 18" square multicolored print referring to the General Instructions. Bind edges of sweatshirt and sleeves referring to the General Instructions. ◄

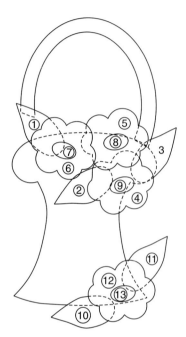

Figure 2
Layer pieces in numerical order as shown.

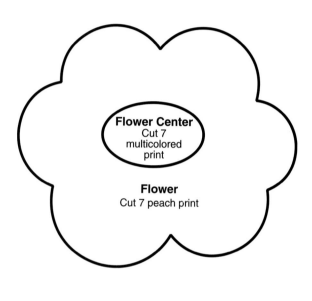

Flower Center
Cut 7
multicolored
print

Flower
Cut 7 peach print

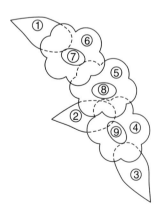

Figure 3
Layer pieces in numerical
order as shown.

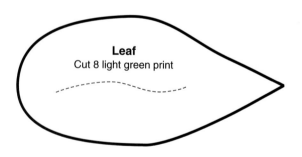

Leaf
Cut 8 light green print

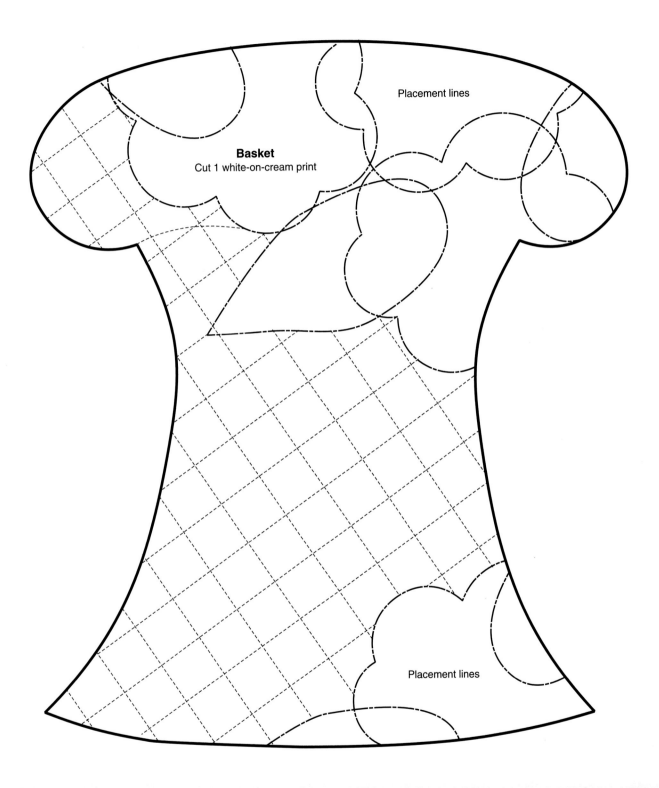

Basket
Cut 1 white-on-cream print

Placement lines

Placement lines

Crazy-Patch Jacket and Skirt

By Charlyne Stewart

Dress up a plain black skirt with the addition of color in a crazy-patch design. Top it with a matching cardigan-style jacket.

Project Note

Use a commercial jacket pattern without darts or button front. Fabric scraps are arranged and stitched on the black lining fabric as a foundation. The jacket is then constructed with no lining. If you prefer to add lining, it would add bulk and weight to the finished jacket.

Project Specifications

Skill Level: Intermediate

Jacket Size: Size varies

Skirt Size: Size varies

Materials

- Commercial jacket pattern with no darts
- Black skirt
- Solid black lining fabric as listed with pattern
- Large pieces of bright-colored scraps
- 2 1/2 yards self-made or purchased black bias binding
- 1 spool each color of your choice and black all-purpose thread
- Basic sewing supplies and tools

Instructions

Step 1. Cut out jacket pieces from black solid lining fabric using commercial pattern. *Note: If pattern has facings for a button front, eliminate them when cutting.*

Step 2. Choose fabric patches from the large pieces of bright-colored scraps. Fold under edges of each piece 1/4" all around; press.

Step 3. Arrange pressed scrap pieces on each lining piece, overlapping edges to leave no black lining showing. Using any color all-purpose thread in the top of the machine and black all-purpose thread in the bobbin and a narrow zigzag stitch, stitch over all edges of all pieces as shown in Figure 1.

Crazy-Patch Jacket and Crasy-Patch Skirt
Placement Diagram
Size Varies

Step 4. Stitch or serge around edges of each crazy-patch jacket section to finish edges.

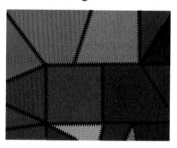

Figure 1
Zigzag stitch over all pressed edges as shown.

Step 5. Assemble jacket referring to pattern instructions.

Step 6. Bind raw edges of jacket and sleeves using self-made or purchased black binding referring to the General Instructions.

Step 7. Cut two strips black solid 1 1/2" x 9". Fold each strip as shown in Figure 2; press and fold in short ends. Hand- or machine-stitch along length to make ties. Tie an overhand knot on one end of each strip. Position unknotted end of each tie on one front edge as desired.

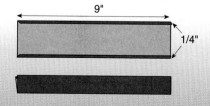

9"

1/4"

Figure 2
Fold 1 1/2" x 9" strips black solid as shown to make ties.

Hand-stitch in place on inside binding edge to finish.

Step 8. Add patches around bottom edge of skirt about 2" up from edge as in Step 3, overlapping pieces as desired. Stitch straight lines through pieces as shown in Figure 3 to add a pattern, if desired. ▥

Figure 3
Straight-stitch lines through pieces
to make a pattern as shown.

Quilt Block Vest and Tote

By Johanna Wilson

Three very familiar star blocks set on-point become a triple flower for the back of a vest when stems and leaves are added. A single block set on-point creates a pocket for the complementary tote bag for carrying shopping or quilting necessities.

Quilt Block Vest
Placement Diagram
Size Varies

Quilt Block Tote
Placement Diagram
15 1/2" x 14 1/4" x 1 1/2"

Star Lily
12" x 12" Block

Star
8 1/2" x 8 1/2" Block

Project Specifications

Skill Level: Intermediate

Vest Size: Size varies

Tote Size: 15 1/2" x 14 1/4" x 1 1/2"

Block Size: 8 1/2" x 8 1/2" and 12" x 12"

Number of Blocks: 1 each size

Materials

- Tan commercial vest
- 8" square burgundy check
- 12" square green print
- 1/2 yard cream solid
- 1 yard tan-on-cream print
- Scraps of a variety of burgundy prints
- 3 yards self-made burgundy/cream plaid bias binding
- 1 piece each batting 10" x 10" and 14" x 14"
- All-purpose thread to match fabrics
- 1 1/2 yards tan 1"-wide cotton or nylon webbing
- 1" piece 7/8"-wide hook-and-loop tape
- Basic sewing supplies and tools, rotary cutter, mat and ruler

Instructions

Step 1. Cut the following from tan-on-cream print: 16 1/2" x 31 1/2" piece for tote lining; 14" x 14" square for Star Lily block backing; 10" x 10" square for Star block backing; 6 1/2" x 6 1/2" square for F; two 3 1/2" x 3 1/2" squares for E; fifteen 2" x 3 1/2" rectangles for C; and nine 2" x 2" squares for D.

Step 2. Cut 32 squares burgundy print scraps 2" x 2" for B and two 5 1/8" x 5 1/8" squares cut in half on one diagonal for G. Cut four 3 1/2" x 3 1/2" squares burgundy check for A.

Step 3. To piece one Star Lily block, place a B square on one end of C; sew on the diagonal as shown in Figure 1; repeat for second B square, again referring to Figure 1.

Step 4. Cut 1/4" from seams; fold back B pieces to complete one B-C unit as shown in Figure 2; repeat for 12 units.

Figure 1
Sew on the diagonal of B;
repeat with second B square.

Figure 2
Cut 1/4" from seams;
fold B pieces back to
complete 1 B-C unit.

Step 5. Sew D to each end of one B-C unit as shown in Figure 3. Sew B-C-D unit to one side of F referring to Figure 4 for placement.

Figure 3
Sew D to each end of a B-C unit.

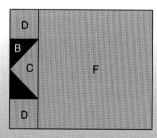

Figure 4
Sew a B-C-D unit to 1 side of F.

Step 6. Sew C to one end of one B-C unit and D to the opposite end as shown in Figure 5; sew to the B-C-D-F unit, again referring to Figure 5.

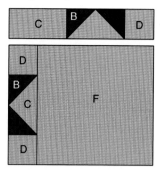

Figure 5
Sew C to 1 end of 1 B-C unit
and D to the opposite end;
sew to the B-C-D-F unit.

Step 7. Cut the 12" x 12" square green print on the diagonal. Cut three 1"-wide bias strips from one half as shown in Figure 6. Fold strips in half along length with wrong sides together; stitch a 1/8" seam. Position seam of shorter pieces at intersection of B-C points on the B-C-D-F unit as shown in Figure 7. Fold stems over raw edges as shown in Figure 8; press.

Figure 6
Cut the 12" x 12" square green
print on the diagonal; cut three
1"-wide bias strips.

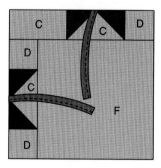

Figure 7
Position seams of shorter bias
pieces at intersection of B-C unit.

Step 8. Starting at the upper corner of B-C-D unit, position the longest strip with seam aligned with corner. Fold over to cover raw edge; hand-stitch in place. Trim shorter stems to fit under center stem as you stitch. End center stem at bottom corner of F square at a 45-degree

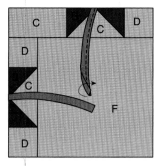

Figure 8
Fold over to cover raw edge.

angle. Hand-stitch shorter stems in place. *Note: By curving as you stitch, the stems will all be different and, as in nature, slight variations are quite acceptable and easier to do.*

Step 9. Prepare template for leaf shape; cut as directed, adding a seam allowance for hand appliqué when cutting. Hand-stitch in place on center stem referring to the Placement Diagram for positioning suggestions.

Step 10. Sew three B-C units to three A squares referring to Figure 9. Sew three D squares to one end of three B-C units as shown in Figure 10.

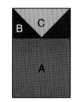

Figure 9
Sew 1 B-C unit to
1 A square.

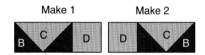

Figure 10
Sew 3 D squares to 1 end of 3 B-C units.

Step 11. Join a B-C-A unit with a B-C-D unit as shown in Figure 11; repeat for three units.

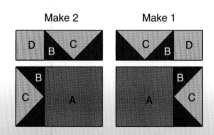

Figure 11
Join 3 B-C-A units with 3 B-C-D units as shown.

Step 12. Place a B square on one corner of E; sew on the diagonal. Trim 1/4" from seam; press. Repeat on

opposite corners and then remaining corners to complete one B-E unit; repeat for two units. Sew C to one side of each B-E unit; press.

Step 13. Arrange pieced units as shown in Figure 12, join to complete one Star Lily block.

Figure 12
Arrange pieced units as shown to complete 1 Star Lily block.

Step 14. Layer pieced block with 14" x 14" batting and backing squares; pin or baste layers together. Hand- or machine-quilt as desired.

Step 15. Bind with self-made burgundy/cream plaid bias binding.

Step 16. Center block on-point on backside of vest; pin or baste in place. Machine-stitch in place close to binding seam to finish.

Step 17. To make one Star block for tote, complete four B-C units referring to Steps 3 and 4. Sew a B-C unit to opposite sides of A. Sew D to each end of the remaining two B-C units; sew to the A-B-C unit. Sew G to each side of the pieced unit to complete one Star block as shown in Figure 13.

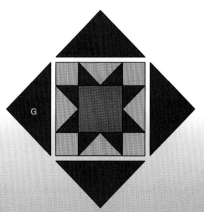

Figure 13
Sew G to each side of the pieced unit to complete 1 Star block.

Step 18. Layer and finish block as in Steps 14 and 15; set aside.

Step 19. Cut one piece cream solid 16 1/2" x 32 1/2" for bag; press under 1/4" along short ends. Press under another 1" on each short end.

Step 20. Position completed Star block on pressed bag piece 3" from one folded edge and equal distance from each side. Stitch in the ditch of the block beside binding down one side, across the bottom and up the other side, backstitching at the beginning and end to secure for pocket.

Step 21. Fold bag piece in half with right sides together; sew a 1/2" seam on sides. To create a flat bottom, with right sides together, fold a corner with seam centered as shown in Figure 14; sew a diagonal line 1 1/2" from end again referring to Figure 14; turn right side out.

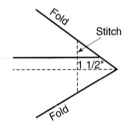

Figure 14
Fold corner with seam centered;
sew a diagonal line 1 1/2" from end.

Step 22. Cut two 24" pieces from tan 1"-wide webbing. Pin one piece on inside of bag at top 3 1/2" from side seams; repeat with remaining piece on opposite side of bag. Sew two rows of stitching 1/4" apart along bottom of fold, catching handles securely in the stitching.

Step 23. Press under 1/2" along short edges of 16 1/2" x 31 1/2" lining piece.

Step 24. Cut one piece cream solid 4 1/2" x 7" for inside pocket. Press under 1/4" on all edges; press under another 1/2" on one 7" edge. Topstitch across 7" edge.

Step 25. Center inside pocket on lining fabric 3 1/2" from one folded edge; stitch three sides to the lining, reinforcing at the top corners.

Step 26. With right sides of lining fabric together, stitch 1/2" side seams. Stitch 7/8"-wide hook-and-loop closure at the top center on the right side of front and back of lining.

Step 27. Slip lining inside tote bag aligning side seams with inside pocket to back of the bag and top edge 1/4" from the top of the tote. Topstitch along the edge of the lining to attach it to the tote; reinforce the handles at top edge. ◾

Checkerboard Star Vest and Purse

By Holly Daniels

Make a coordinated vest and purse in bright colors to showcase your quilting talents.

Checkerboard Star Vest
Placement Diagram
Size Varies

Fifty-Four Forty or Fight
6" x 6" Block

Project Notes

The sample vest was made using Simplicity pattern 8744 in medium. If this pattern number has been discontinued, look for a vest pattern with a similar style using no darts. There is always a vest pattern available in this style but the numbers do frequently change.

If you make a larger or smaller vest, adjust the number of Four-Patch units and single squares accordingly in Step 1.

Project Specifications

Skill Level: Intermediate

Vest Size: Size varies

Purse Size: 6 1/2" x 6 1/2" (includes binding)

Block Size: 6" x 6"

Number of Blocks: 3 for vest, 1 for purse

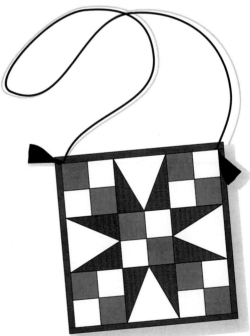

Checkerboard Star Purse
Placement Diagram
6 1/2" x 6 1/2"
(includes binding)

Materials

- Commercial vest pattern
- Scraps of assorted red and black prints
- Scraps white, off-white, cream and light gray prints
- Lining fabric as indicated on vest pattern
- 2 squares lining fabric 6 1/2" x 6 1/2"
- 2 squares thin quilt batting 6 1/2" x 6 1/2"

- 3 yards self-made or purchased binding
- All-purpose thread to match fabrics
- 1 1/2 yards black rayon cord
- 2 (1 1/2") black rayon tassels
- Basic sewing supplies and tools and rotary cutter, ruler and mat

Instructions

Step 1. Cut each scrap fabric into 1 1/2" x 1 1/2" squares. You will need 526 dark squares and 486 light squares. Join two light and two dark squares to make a Four-Patch unit as shown in Figure 1; repeat for 213 units, leaving remaining squares unjoined. ***Note:*** *If scraps are large enough to cut 1 1/2" x 42" strips, join a light and dark strip along length with right sides together; cut into 1 1/2" segments as shown in Figure 2. Repeat to cut 426 segments. Join segments as shown in Figure 1 to make Four-Patch units.*

Figure 1
Join 2 light and 2 dark
squares to make a
Four-Patch unit as shown.

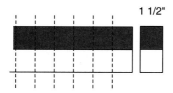

Figure 2
Cut strips into 1 1/2"
segments as shown.

Step 2. Prepare templates using patterns given. Cut as directed on each piece for one block.

Step 3. To piece one Fifty-four Forty or Fight block, sew A and AR to B; repeat for four units. Join pieced units with five Four-Patch units to complete one block as shown in Figure 3; press. Repeat for four blocks.

Step 4. Cut two strips each red print 1 1/2" x 6 1/2" and 1 1/2" x 8 1/2". Sew a shorter strip to two opposite sides and the remaining strips to remaining sides as shown in Figure 4; press seams toward strips. Repeat for two of the three remaining blocks.

Figure 3
Join pieced unts with 5 Four-Patch
units to complete 1 block.

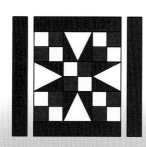

Figure 4
Sew a shorter strip to 2 opposite
sides and the remaining strips to
remaining sides as shown.

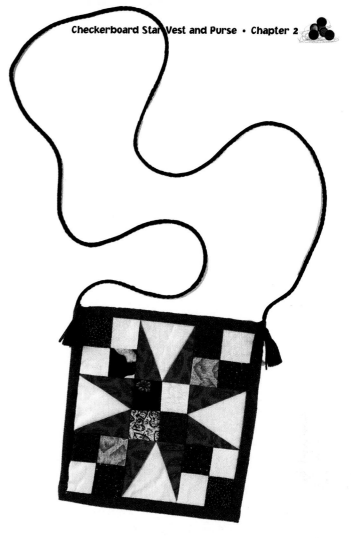

Step 5. Join five each dark and light 1 1/2" x 1 1/2" squares to make a strip as shown in Figure 5; repeat. Repeat for two eight-square strips. Sew the shorter strips to two opposite sides of one pieced-and-bordered block. Sew the longer strips to the remaining sides referring to Figure 6; press seams toward strips.

Figure 5
Join 5 dark and 5 light 1 1/2" x
1 1/2" squares to make a strip.

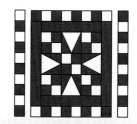

Figure 6
Sew the longer strips to
the remaining sides.

Step 6. Cut two strips each red print 1 1/2" x 10 1/2" and 1 1/2" x 12 1/2". Sew the shorter strips to opposite sides and longer strips to the top and bottom of the block bordered in Step 5; press seams toward strips.

Step 7. To make one vest front, join 50 Four-Patch units with 36 dark and 15 light squares to make units to surround a bordered block as shown in Figure 7; repeat for reverse side of vest front. Press seams in one direction.

Figure 7
Join Four-Patch units and single squares to make units to surround a bordered block as shown.

Step 8. Join pieced units with bordered blocks to complete vest fronts; press. Cut out vest fronts using commercial pattern. ***Note:*** *To insure that the blocks are located in the same place on each vest front, place commercial pattern over first cut side; mark position of block on pattern. Place pattern on second vest front, lining traced block position up with pieced section before cutting.*

Step 9. To make vest back, join 84 Four-Patch units with 10 dark and 12 light squares to make units to surround larger pieced-and-bordered block made in Step 6 referring to Figure 8. Join pieced units with bordered block to complete vest back. Cut out vest back using commercial pattern.

Figure 8
Join Four-Patch units and single squares to make units to surround larger pieced-and-bordered block.

Step 10. Finish vest with lining referring to commercial pattern, binding armholes and outside edges of vest with self-made or purchased binding to finish.

Step 11. To make purse back, join nine Four-Patch units as shown in Figure 9; press seams in one direction.

Figure 9
To make purse back, join 9 Four-Patch units as shown.

Step 12. Layer one 6 1/2" x 6 1/2" lining square right sides together with purse back and one 6 1/2" x 6 1/2" piece thin quilt batting; baste edges together. Repeat with remaining pieced block.

Step 13. Cut a 7" piece of self-made or prepared binding; apply to one edge of each layered and basted section referring to the General Instructions. Trim excess at ends as shown in Figure 10.

Step 14. Layer purse sections with lining sides together and bound edges matching. Lay black rayon cord along raw edges around unbound sides as shown in Figure 11; whipstitch in place. Apply self-made or purchased binding to sides and bottom, enclosing cord ends. Hand-stitch tassels to top corners to finish. ◼

Figure 10
Trim excess binding at ends.

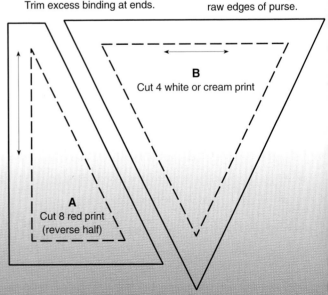

Figure 11
Place cord along raw edges of purse.

B
Cut 4 white or cream print

A
Cut 8 red print
(reverse half)

Autumn Glory Cardigan

By Beth Wheeler

Dress up for the autumn season in this warm cardigan sweatshirt.

Autumn Glory Cardigan
Placement Diagram
Size Varies

Project Specifications

Skill Level: Beginner

Cardigan Size: Size varies

Materials

- Bittersweet sweatshirt with set-in or raglan sleeves
- Print scraps as follows: brown and multicolored red/orange/green
- 18" square gold print
- All-purpose thread to match sweatshirt
- Variegated red/rust/yellow and solid brown and rust rayon thread
- 1/3 yard iron-on fabric stabilizer
- 1/3 yard fusible transfer web
- Basic sewing supplies and tools

Instructions

Step 1. Cut sweatshirt down the center front. Cut off neck ribbing and hemline ribbing. Remove sleeve cuffs and cut sleeves to desired length. Round bottom and neck corners on front sides as shown in Figure 1.

Figure 1
Round corners on
sweatshirt fronts.

and referring to the pattern pieces for number to cut. Cut out shapes, leaving a margin around each one.

Step 4. Fuse cut shapes to the wrong side of fabric scraps referring to the pattern pieces for color. Cut out shapes on traced lines; remove paper backing.

Step 5. Position shapes in place on sweatshirt left and right fronts referring to the Placement Diagram and photo of project for positioning suggestions and to Figure 2 for numerical order; fuse in place.

Figure 2
Layer pieces in numerical order as shown.

Step 2. Prepare 3 yards bias binding using 18" square gold print and bind raw edges of sleeves and sweatshirt referring to the General Instructions.

Step 3. Prepare templates for appliqué shapes using pattern pieces given. Trace shapes onto the paper side of the fusible transfer web, leaving space between shapes

Step 6. Iron pieces of iron-on fabric stabilizer under each area to be appliquéd following manufacturer's instructions.

Step 7. Satin-stitch around each fused shape using rayon thread to match fabrics in the top of the machine and all-purpose thread to match sweatshirt in the bobbin. Repeat with detail lines marked on patterns to finish. ◄

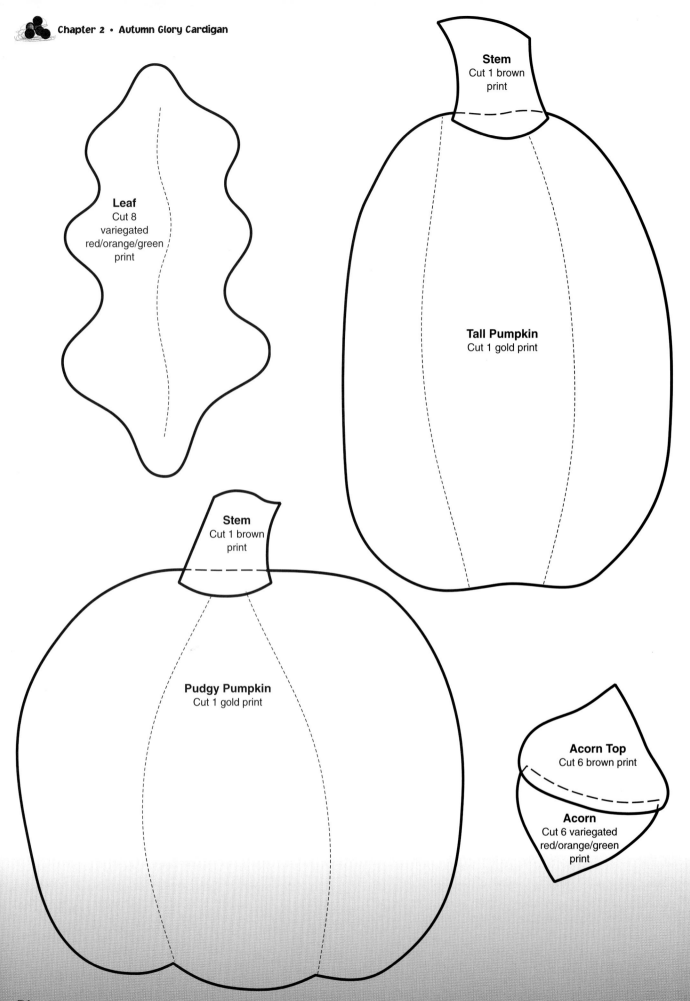

Leaf
Cut 8
variegated
red/orange/green
print

Stem
Cut 1 brown
print

Tall Pumpkin
Cut 1 gold print

Stem
Cut 1 brown
print

Pudgy Pumpkin
Cut 1 gold print

Acorn Top
Cut 6 brown print

Acorn
Cut 6 variegated
red/orange/green
print

Christmas Star Tie

By Karen Neary

Foundation-piecing makes construction of this tiny block with its long points a cinch. Stitch up a few for the men and boys in your life.

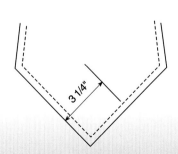

Christmas Star
3" x 3" Block

Christmas Star Tie
Placement Diagram
Size Varies

Project Note

Purchase a commercial tie pattern. Use the tie tip pattern given to adjust commercial pattern to fit patchwork. Prepare patchwork or appliqué sections before constructing tie as instructed on commercial pattern.

Project Specifications

Skill Level: Intermediate

Tie Size: Size Varies

Block Size: 3" x 3"

Number of Blocks: 1

Materials

- Scraps red and green prints
- Commercial pattern for adult-size tie
- Cream Christmas print fabric for tie and lining and notions as listed on pattern
- All-purpose thread to match fabrics
- Gold metallic thread
- 5"-length 1/2"-wide off-white satin ribbon
- 10" x 10" square tear-off fabric stabilizer
- Basic sewing supplies and tools and fade-out pen

Instructions

Step 1. Trace patterns for Christmas Star block onto the 10" x 10" piece of tear-off fabric stabilizer. Cut fabric scraps larger than shapes on pattern. Pin piece 1 onto unmarked side of one marked stabilizer base. Place piece 2 right sides together with piece 1; on marked side of stabilizer, stitch on line between pieces 1 and 2.

Step 2. Press piece 2 open; trim 1/4" from seam lines, if necessary. Place piece 3 right sides together with piece 2. Stitch as in Step 3; press piece 3 open. Continue adding pieces in numerical order until all pieces have been added.

Step 3. Trim stitched sections to size of stabilizer base. Join A and B sections as shown in Figure 1 to complete block.

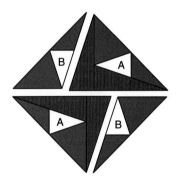

Figure 1
Join A and B sections
to complete block.

Step 4. Stitch in the ditch of seams using gold metallic thread in the top of the machine and all-purpose thread in the bobbin. Carefully remove stabilizer.

Step 5. Cut pieces for tie using commercial pattern combined with tie tip pattern given.

Step 6. Using fade-out pen, draw a line 3 1/4" up from and parallel to the left side of point as shown in Figure 2.

Step 7. With right side of stitched block facing up, fold under seam allowance on the top left side as shown in Figure 3; press. Fold under seam allowance on top right side; press to mark seam line.

Figure 2
Mark tip of tie as shown.

3 1/4"

Fold

Figure 3
Press seam allowance
under on top left side.

Step 8. Lay block right side up in position on tie; flip block back along the right seam allowance so that the

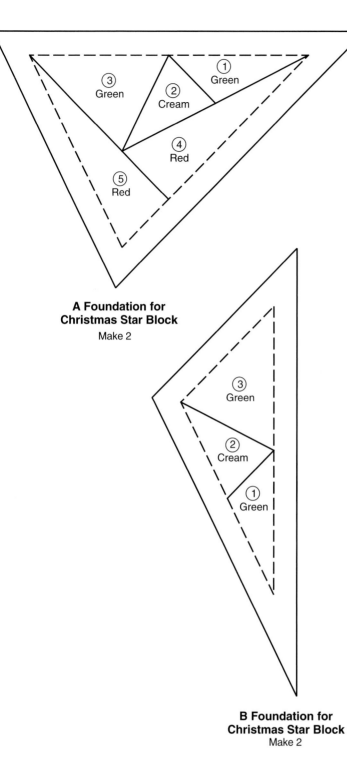

**A Foundation for
Christmas Star Block**
Make 2

③ Green

② Cream

① Green

④ Red

⑤ Red

③ Green

② Cream

① Green

**B Foundation for
Christmas Star Block**
Make 2

right side of the block is facing the right side of the tie. Pressed seam line on block should be aligned with line drawn on tie front in Step 2. Stitch across this seam.

Step 9. Fold block back down; press. Hand-stitch pressed left side of block to tie.

Step 10. Finish tie as instructed with commercial tie pattern making loop using 5"-length 1/2"-wide off-white satin ribbon. ◀

Tie Tip Pattern
Adjust commercial pattern to fit this
pattern to complete tie to fit a 3" x 3"
block on the tip.

Snowed Under Tie

By Karen Neary

Make this neat snowman-design tie for wearing on a cold winter's day.

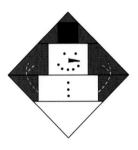

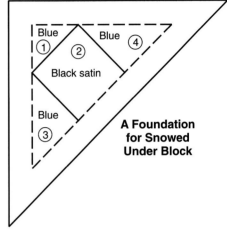

Step 2. Before lining and removing tear-off stabilizer, machine-stitch nose using orange machine-embroidery thread in the top of the machine and all-purpose thread in the bobbin and a narrow-to-wider satin stitch; repeat with black machine-embroidery thread and a small satin stitch for eyes, five mouth marks and three button marks on Snowman center and silver machine-embroidery thread and a narrow zigzag stitch for arms.

Step 3. Finish tie as for Christmas Star Tie. ◼

Snowed Under
3" x 3" Block

Snowed Under
Placement Diagram
Size Varies

A Foundation for Snowed Under Block

B Foundation for Snowed Under Block

C Foundation for Snowed Under Block

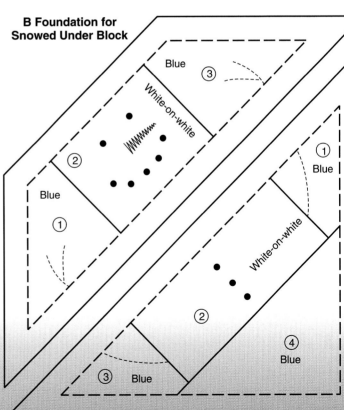

Project Specifications

Skill Level: Intermediate

Tie Size: Size Varies

Block Size: 3" x 3"

Number of Blocks: 1

Materials

- Scraps white-on-white print
- 2" x 2" square black satin
- Commercial pattern for adult-size tie
- Blue dot fabric for tie and lining and notions as listed on pattern
- All-purpose thread to match fabrics
- Black, orange and silver machine-embroidery thread
- 5"-length 1/2"-wide blue satin ribbon
- 6" x 6" square tear-off fabric stabilizer
- Basic sewing supplies and tools and fade-out pen

Instructions

Step 1. Complete tie referring to the instructions for the Christmas Star Tie on page 58 except mark position of nose, mouth, arms and other marks on block using fade-out pen.

Pick o' the Irish Tie

By Karen Neary

Dress up for Saint Patrick's Day using this appliquéd shamrock pattern and simple strip piecing.

Pick o' the Irish
3" x 3" Block

Pick o' the Irish
Placement Diagram
Size Varies

Project Specifications

Skill Level: Intermediate

Tie Size: Size Varies

Block Size: 3" x 3"

Number of Blocks: 1

Materials

- 3 1/2" x 3 1/2" square white-on-white print
- Scraps red, orange, yellow, green, blue and violet solids
- Commercial pattern for adult-size tie
- Green solid fabric for tie and lining and notions as listed on pattern
- All-purpose thread to match fabrics
- Green machine-embroidery thread
- 5"-length 1/2"-wide green satin ribbon
- 3" x 3" square fusible transfer web
- 3 1/2" x 3 1/2" square tear-off fabric stabilizer
- Basic sewing supplies and tools and fade-out pen

Instructions

Step 1. Trace shamrock shape onto paper side of 3" x 3" square fusible transfer web. Fuse to wrong side of green solid. Cut out shape on traced line; remove paper backing.

Step 2. *Fuse shape to the center of the 3 1/2" x 3 1/2" white-on-white print square referring to manufacturer's instructions.*

Step 3. Mark lines from foundation pattern onto the 3 1/2" x 3 1/2" square tear-off fabric stabilizer. Place under 3 1/2" x 3 1/2" white-on-white print square with marked lines on bottom.

Step 4. Using green machine-embroidery thread in the top of the machine and all-purpose thread in the bobbin, satin-stitch shamrock shape in place, adding stem and leaf lines as indicated on pattern piece.

Shamrock
Cut 1 green solid

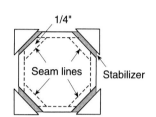

Figure 1
Trim white-on-white print square 1/4" beyond strip seam line as shown.

Step 5. Trim white-on-white print square 1/4" beyond seam lines of first stripe on each corner as shown in Figure 1. Foundation-piece block corners referring to Steps 1 and 2 of the instructions for the Christmas Star Tie on page 58.

Step 6. Trim stitched square even with stabilizer base. Complete remainder of tie referring to Steps 5–10 for the Christmas Star Tie.

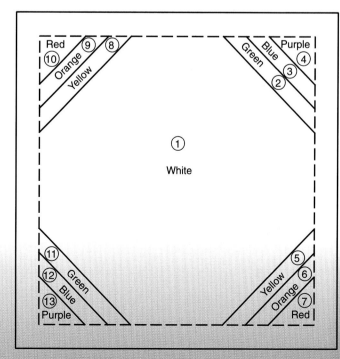

Foundation for Pick o' the Irish Block

Hearts in the Pines begins on page 64.

Chapter 3
Quilting All Around

Quilts may have started out on beds only, but now you can make lovely scrap projects to coordinate with every room in your home. Whether you make just one project from the sets given or stitch the entire set, you'll enjoy using your fabric scraps to decorate your home with quilting.

In This Chapter

Hearts in the Pines

By Kate Laucomer

Flying Geese units combine to make the Pine Tree designs on this pillow and wall quilt set.

Heart
6" x 6" Block

Tree
6" x 6" Block

Wall Quilt

Project Specifications

Skill Level: Beginner

Project Size: 19 1/2" x 25 1/2"

Block Size: 6" x 6"

Number of Blocks: 3 each design

Materials

- 3 squares assorted tan prints 6 1/2" x 6 1/2"
- Scraps red, tan and green prints
- 5" x 5" square brown print
- 1/8 yard dark tan print
- Backing 23" x 29"
- Batting 23" x 29"
- 3 yards self-made or purchased binding
- Neutral color all-purpose thread
- Black 6-strand embroidery floss
- 1/4 yard fusible transfer web
- Basic sewing supplies and tools

Instructions

Step 1. Prepare template for heart shape using pattern given. Trace 12 hearts on the paper side of the fusible transfer web. Cut out each shape leaving a margin all around.

Step 2. Fuse each heart shape to the wrong side of red print scraps. Cut out shapes; remove paper backing.

Hearts in the Pines Wall Quilt
Placement Diagram
19 1/2" x 25 1/2"

Step 3. Fold each tan print square in half on each diagonal; crease to mark centers and unfold.

Step 4. Position a heart on each diagonal line 1/2" from center mark on each tan print square as shown in Figure 1; fuse in place.

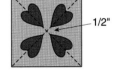
1/2"

Figure 1
Place a heart shape
on each diagonal
line 1/2" from center.

Step 5. Using 3 strands black embroidery floss, blanket-stitch around each heart shape. ***Note:*** *If your machine will make a buttonhole stitch, add black thread of your favorite type to your list of materials and machine-stitch all appliqué shapes in place.* Set aside appliquéd squares.

Step 6. Cut 18 rectangles from a variety of green print scraps 2" x 3 1/2" for A.

Step 7. Cut 36 squares from a variety of tan print scraps 2" x 2" for B.

Step 8. Place a B square right sides together on an A rectangle as shown in Figure 2; sew on the diagonal of the square, again referring to Figure 2.

B

Figure 2
Place a B square on A and
stitch on 1 diagonal as shown.

Step 9. Trim excess layers 1/4" beyond stitched line as shown in Figure 3. Press B back as shown in Figure 4.

Figure 3
Trim excess 1/4" beyond stitched line.

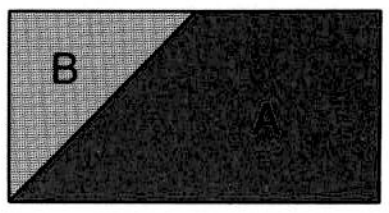

Figure 4
Press B back as shown.

Step 10. Repeat on opposite corner of A with a second B square; trim and press as in Step 9 to complete one Flying Geese unit as shown in Figure 5. Repeat for 18 Flying Geese units.

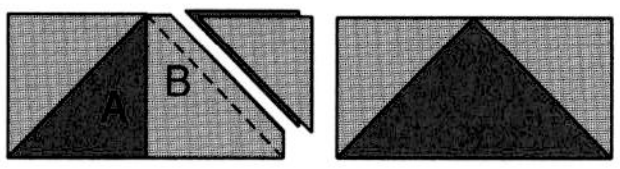

Figure 5
Sew a second B to A, trim and press to make 1 Flying Geese unit.

Step 11. Cut 12 assorted tan print and six brown print rectangles 1 1/2" x 2" for C. Sew a brown print C between two tan print C's to make a Trunk unit as shown in Figure 6; repeat for six Trunk units.

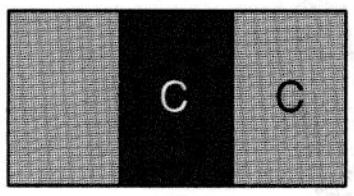

Figure 6
Sew a brown print C between 2 tan print C's to make a Trunk unit.

Step 12. Join three Flying Geese units with one Trunk unit to make a Tree unit as shown in Figure 7; repeat for six Tree units.

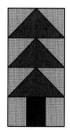
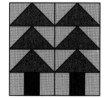

Figure 7
Join 3 Flying Geese units with 1 Trunk unit to make a Tree unit.

Figure 8
Join 2 Tree units to make a Tree block.

Step 13. Join two tree units to make a Tree block as shown in Figure 8; repeat for three blocks.

Step 14. Join two Tree blocks with a Heart block to make a row as shown in Figure 9. Join two Heart blocks with one Tree block to make a row, again referring to Figure 9; press seams in one direction.

Step 15. Join the two rows to complete pieced center; press seam open.

Figure 9
Join blocks to make 2 different rows as shown.

Step 16. Cut two strips each dark tan print 1 1/4" x 18 1/2" and 1 1/4" x 14". Sew the longer strips to opposite long sides and the shorter strips to the top and bottom of the pieced center; press seams toward strips.

Step 17. Cut 52 rectangles from assorted green print scraps 2" x 3 1/2" and 104 squares from assorted tan print scraps 2" x 2". Make 52 Flying Geese units referring to Steps 8–10.

Step 18. Join 13 Flying Geese units to make a strip as shown in Figure 10; press seams in one direction. Repeat for four strips. Sew a strip to opposite long sides of the pieced center; press seams toward strips. Sew the remaining strips to the top and bottom; press seams toward strips.

Figure 10
Join 13 Flying Geese units to make a strip.

Step 19. Finish quilt referring to the General Instructions.

Hearts & Geese Pillow

Project Specifications

Skill Level: Beginner

Project Size: 12" x 12"

Block Size: 6" x 6"

Number of Blocks: 1

Materials

- 6 1/2" x 6 1/2" square tan print
- Scraps of assorted red, tan and green prints
- Muslin 14" x 14"
- Backing 14" x 16"
- Batting 14" x 14"

Hearts & Geese Pillow
Placement Diagram
12" x 12"

- 1 1/2 yards self-made or purchased binding
- Neutral color all-purpose thread
- Black 6-strand embroidery floss
- Polyester fiberfill or 12" x 12" pillow form
- 1/4 yard fusible transfer web
- Basic sewing supplies and tools

Instructions

Step 1. Prepare one Heart block referring to Steps 1–5 for Wall Quilt.

Step 2. Cut 24 rectangles from a variety of green print scraps 2" x 3 1/2" for A.

Step 3. Cut 48 squares from a variety of tan print scraps 2" x 2" for B.

Step 4. Make 24 Flying Geese units referring to Steps 8–10 for Wall Quilt.

Step 5. Join four Flying Geese units to make a strip; repeat. Sew a strip to opposite sides of the Heart block with each strip going in a different direction as shown in Figure 11; press seams toward strips.

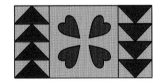

Figure 11
Sew a strip to opposite sides of the Heart block
with each strip going in a different direction.

Step 6. Join six Flying Geese units to make a strip. Sew two Flying Geese units to one end going in a different direction as shown in Figure 12; repeat for a second strip. Sew these strips to the remaining sides of the Heart block referring to Figure 13 to finish pillow top.

Figure 12
Sew 2 Flying Geese units to 1
end going in a different direction.

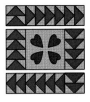

Figure 13
Sew these strips to
the remaining sides
of the Heart block.

Step 7. Sandwich batting between completed pillow top and the 14" x 14" muslin square; pin or baste layers together to hold. Quilt as desired by hand or machine. *Note: The pillow shown was machine-quilted in the ditch of seams and around heart shapes.* When quilting is complete, trim edges even.

Step 8. Fold pillow backing piece in half with right sides together bringing 14" edges together; cut along folded edge to make two 8" x 14" pieces. Sew along cut edge with a 1/2" seam allowance, leaving a 4"–6" opening as shown in Figure 14; press seam open.

Step 9. Place stitched backing piece wrong sides together with quilted pillow top; trim backing piece even with pillow top.

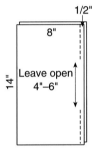

Figure 14
Sew along cut edge with a
1/2" seam allowance, leaving
a 4"–6" opening as shown.

Step 10. Bind edges with self-made or purchased binding referring to the General Instructions.

Step 11. Stuff pillow through opening in backing, using polyester fiberfill or a 12" x 12" pillow form; slipstitch opening closed to finish pillow.

Tree Pillow

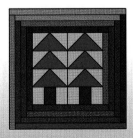

Tree Pillow
Placement Diagram
10" x 10"

Project Specifications

Skill Level: Beginner

Project Size: 10" x 10"

Block Size: 6" x 6"

Number of Blocks: 1

Materials

- Scraps of assorted tan and green print
- 2" x 3" rectangle brown print
- 16 different scrap strips 1" x 10 1/2"
- Muslin 12" x 12"
- Backing 12" x 14"
- Batting 12" x 12"
- 1 1/4 yards self-made or purchased binding
- Neutral color all-purpose thread
- Polyester fiberfill or 10" x 10" pillow form
- Basic sewing supplies and tools

Instructions

Step 1. Cut 6 rectangles from a variety of green print scraps 2" x 3 1/2" for A.

Step 2. Cut 12 squares from a variety of tan print scraps 2" x 2" for B.

Step 3. Make six Flying Geese units referring to Steps 8–10 for Wall Quilt.

Step 4. Cut four assorted tan print and two brown print rectangles 1 1/2" x 2" for C. Sew a brown print C between two tan print C's to make a Trunk unit as shown in Figure 6; repeat for two Trunk units.

Step 5. Join three Flying Geese units with a Trunk unit to make a Tree unit referring to Figure 7; repeat for two Tree units.

Step 6. Join the two Tree units to make a Tree block; press joining seam open.

Step 7. Sew a 1" x 10 1/2" strip to one side of the Tree block; press strip away from block. Trim excess strip even with block as shown in Figure 15.

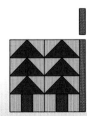

Figure 15
Trim excess strip even
with block as shown.

Step 8. Continue adding strips to adjacent sides of the Tree block in numerical order as shown in Figure 16 until there are four strips on each side of the block. Press seam away from block and trim excess strip even with block after stitching each strip.

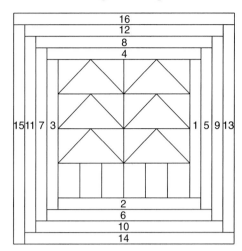

Figure 16
Sew strips to Tree block in
numerical order as shown.

Step 9. Sandwich batting between completed pillow top and the 12" x 12" muslin square; pin or baste layers together to hold. Quilt as desired by hand or machine. *Note: The pillow shown was machine-quilted in the ditch of seams.* When quilting is complete, trim edges even.

Step 10. Finish pillow as in Steps 8–11 for Hearts & Geese Pillow.

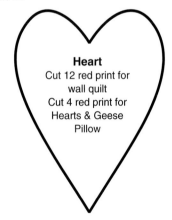

Heart
Cut 12 red print for
wall quilt
Cut 4 red print for
Hearts & Geese
Pillow

I Love the Blues

By Connie Kauffman

Four blocks form the basis for this tablecloth quilt. This is a fun project that lets you use all those blue fabrics you love in one quilt. Make four chair pads to match using a different block in each one.

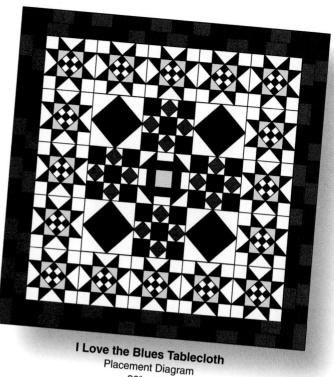

I Love the Blues Tablecloth
Placement Diagram
36" x 36"

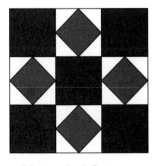

Diamonds & Squares
6" x 6" Block
Make 4 for Tablecloth
Make 1 for Chair Pad

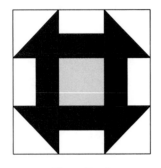

Churn Dash
6" x 6" Block
Make 1 for Tablecloth
Make 1 for Chair Pad

Nine-Patch Star
6" x 6" Block
Make 16 for Tablecloth
Make 1 for Chair Pad

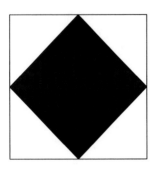

Square in a Square
6" x 6" Block
Make 4 for Tablecloth
Make 1 for Chair Pad

Instructions are given for the tablecloth and four chair pads. The chair pads each have a different block in the center. If you plan to make the set, it is easier to cut out the required pieces and stitch the blocks for both at the same time. Separate Materials list and Instructions are given along with instructions to piece each block.

Tablecloth

Project Specifications
Skill Level: Intermediate
Project Size: 36" x 36"
Block Size: 6" x 6"
Number of Blocks: 25

Materials
- 1/2 yard total assorted light blue prints
- 3/4 yard total assorted medium blue prints
- 3/4 yard total assorted dark blue prints
- 1 yard white-on-white print
- Backing 40" x 40"
- Thin batting 40" x 40"
- 4 1/2 yards self-made or purchased navy blue binding
- All-purpose thread to match fabrics
- Basic sewing supplies and tools

Project Notes

These projects use a wide variety of blue fabrics. Pull out your blue fabrics and sort them in piles of light, medium and dark. I chose to use five different light and medium blue prints and seven different dark blue prints. The background is white-on-white print.

Making Blocks

Step 1. Prepare templates using pattern pieces given. Cut as directed on each piece for one block. *Note: These instructions are given to piece one block; project instructions dictate the number of each block needed for each specific project.*

Step 2. To piece one Square in a Square block, sew a white-on-white print B to each side of a medium blue print A as shown in Figure 1.

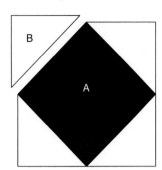

Figure 1
Piece 1 Square in a
Square block as shown.

Step 3. To piece one Churn Dash block, sew a white-on-white print E to a dark blue print E; repeat for four units. Sew a white-on-white print D to a dark blue print D; repeat for four units. Arrange the pieced units with a light blue print C as shown in Figure 2 to make rows; join pieced units in rows. Join rows and press to complete one block.

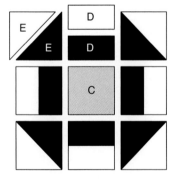

Figure 2
Piece 1 Churn Dash
block as shown.

Step 4. To piece one Diamonds & Squares block, sew G to each side of a medium blue print F; repeat for four units. Arrange the F-G units with the dark blue print C squares in rows. Join the units in rows as shown in Figure 3; join rows and press to complete one block.

Step 5. To piece one Nine-Patch Star block, sew a medium blue print J to each side of a white-on-white print J; repeat. Sew a white-on-white print J to each side of a medium blue print J. Join the J units to make a Nine-Patch unit as shown in Figure 4.

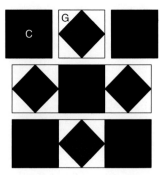

Figure 3
Piece 1 Diamonds &
Squares block as shown.

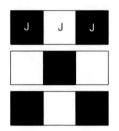

Figure 4
Join units to make
a Nine-Patch unit.

Step 6. Sew a light blue print H to each side of the Nine-Patch unit. Sew a dark blue print H to adjacent short sides of I; repeat for four units.

Step 7. Arrange K squares and H-I units and the Nine-Patch unit to make rows as shown in Figure 5; join units to make rows. Join rows to complete one block; press.

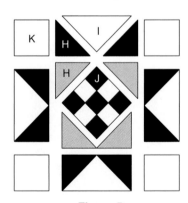

Figure 5
Piece 1 Nine-Patch
Star block as shown.

Making Tablecloth

Step 1. Make 16 Nine-Patch Star blocks, four each Square in a Square and Diamonds & Squares blocks and one Churn Dash block referring to Making Blocks instructions.

Step 2. Arrange the pieced blocks in five rows of five blocks each referring to Figure 6. Join blocks in rows; join rows to complete the pieced center. Press seams in one direction.

Figure 6
Arrange blocks in 5 rows of 5 blocks each.

Step 3. Cut leftover medium and dark blue print 2"-wide strips from 3 1/2" to 5" long. Mix up fabrics and piece two strips each 2" x 30 1/2" and 2" x 33 1/2". Sew the shorter pieced strips to the top and bottom and longer strips to opposite sides of the pieced center; press seams toward strips.

Step 4. Repeat Step 3 to make two strips each 2" x 33 1/2" and 2" x 36 1/2". Sew the shorter pieced strips to the top and bottom and longer strips to opposite sides of the pieced center; press seams toward strips.

Step 5. Prepare pieced top for quilting and finish referring to the General Instructions. *Note: The tablecloth shown used the quilting design given in the centers of the Square in a Square blocks and was quilted in the ditch of remaining pieces as shown in Figure 7.*

Figure 7
Quilt as shown.

Chair Pads

Project Specifications
Skill Level: Intermediate
Chair Pad Size: 14" x 14"
Block Size: 6" x 6"
Number of Blocks: 1 of each design—4 designs

Materials
- 1/4 yard total light blue prints
- 5/8 yard total medium blue prints
- 5/8 yard total dark blue prints
- 1/3 yard white-on-white print
- 1 yard backing fabric
- 1 yard fat batting
- All-purpose thread to match fabrics
- Basic sewing supplies and tools

Instructions
Step 1. Make one block of each design referring to Making Blocks instructions.

Step 2. Cut four strips each medium blue prints: 2 1/2" x 6 1/2" for piece 1, 2 1/2" x 8 1/2" for piece 2, 2 1/2" x 10 1/2" for piece 5 and 2 1/2" x 12 1/2" for piece 6.

Step 3. Cut four strips each dark blue prints: 2 1/2" x 8 1/2"

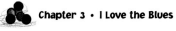

I Love the Blues Chair Pad
Placement Diagram
14" x 14"

I Love the Blues Chair Pad
Placement Diagram
14" x 14"

I Love the Blues Chair Pad
Placement Diagram
14" x 14"

for piece 3, 2 1/2" x 10 1/2" for piece 4, 2 1/2" x 12 1/2" for piece 7 and 2 1/2" x 14 1/2" for piece 8.

Step 4. Sew the strips cut in Steps 2 and 3 to the sides of a pieced square in numerical order referring to Figure 8, pressing seams toward each strip after stitching. Sew strips in same order to each block. ***Note:*** *If your chair is larger than the 14" x 14" finished size of these blocks, continue adding strips in the same color order until you have the correct size. If your seat is wider at the front than the back, measure the seat and taper the block to fit.*

I Love the Blues Chair Pad
Placement Diagram
14" x 14"

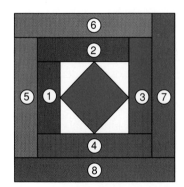

Figure 8
Sew 2 1/2"-wide strips to center block in
numerical order as shown.

Step 5. Use a cup or small bowl to shape and cut round corners as shown in Figure 9.

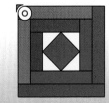

Figure 9
Use a cup or small bowl to
shape and cut round corners.

Step 6. Cut four pieces fat batting 16" x 16" each. Pin a batting piece to the wrong side of each pieced block. Quilt as desired by hand or machine. ***Note:*** *For thicker chair pads, two layers of batting may be used. Machine quilting is recommended if the layers are thick.*

Step 7. When quilting is complete, trim edges even.

Step 8. Cut 16 strips from remaining blue prints 2" x 14 1/2" for ties. Fold each strip along length with right sides together; sew along length and at an angle across one end as shown in Figure 10; trim excess at angle. Turn right side out; press.

Figure 10
Sew folded strip along length and at an angle across 1 end.

Step 9. Pin two tie strips to each back corner of each quilted block as shown in Figure 11, placing ties to fit your chairs. Stitch over ties several times to secure in place.

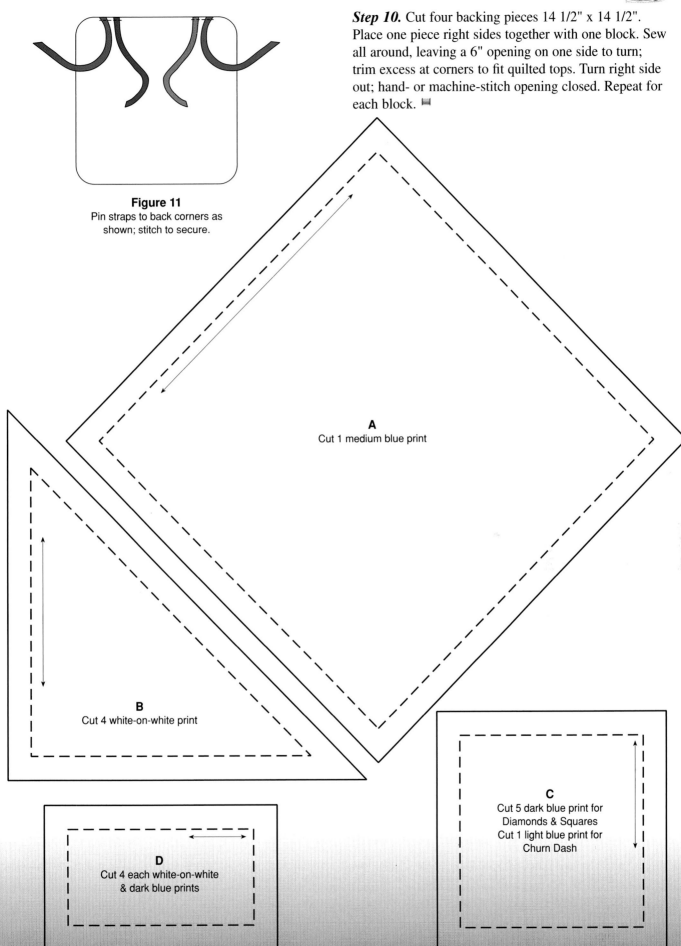

Step 10. Cut four backing pieces 14 1/2" x 14 1/2". Place one piece right sides together with one block. Sew all around, leaving a 6" opening on one side to turn; trim excess at corners to fit quilted tops. Turn right side out; hand- or machine-stitch opening closed. Repeat for each block.

Figure 11
Pin straps to back corners as
shown; stitch to secure.

A
Cut 1 medium blue print

B
Cut 4 white-on-white print

C
Cut 5 dark blue print for
Diamonds & Squares
Cut 1 light blue print for
Churn Dash

D
Cut 4 each white-on-white
& dark blue prints

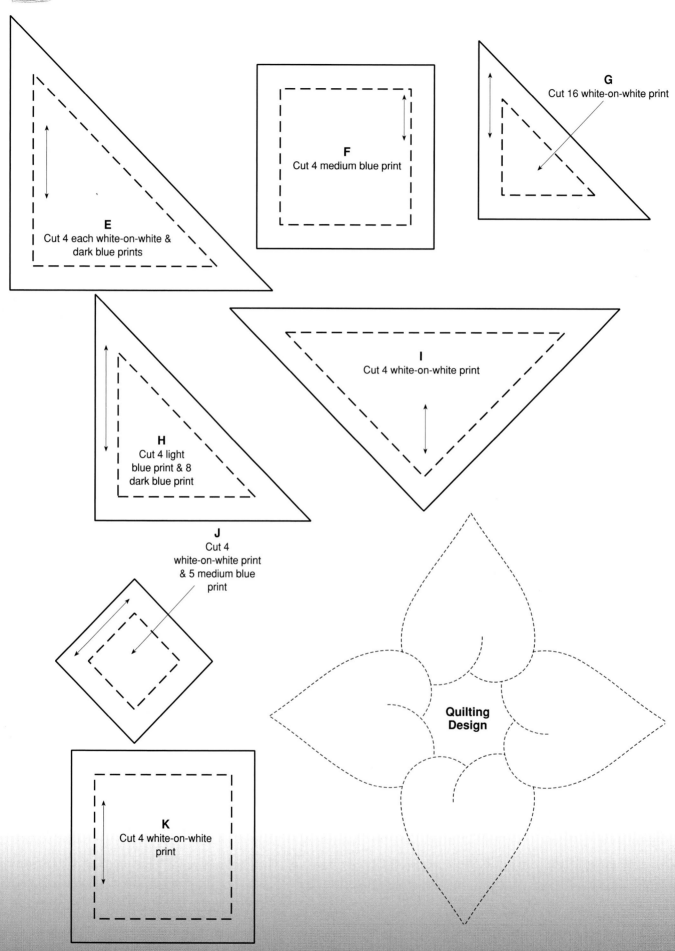

E
Cut 4 each white-on-white &
dark blue prints

F
Cut 4 medium blue print

G
Cut 16 white-on-white print

H
Cut 4 light
blue print & 8
dark blue print

I
Cut 4 white-on-white print

J
Cut 4
white-on-white print
& 5 medium blue
print

K
Cut 4 white-on-white
print

**Quilting
Design**

Rosy Red Apple Kitchen Set

By Marian Shenk

Coordinate your kitchen table, chairs and toaster with this cheery kitchen set.

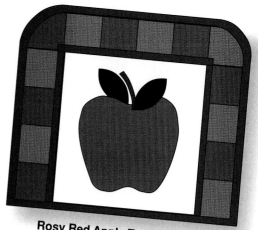

Rosy Red Apple Toaster Cover
Placement Diagram
12" x 10" x 6"

Rosy Red Apple Table Runner
Placement Diagram
14 3/8" x 45 5/8"

Rosy Red Apple Chair Back Pad
Placement Diagram
16" x 22"

Project Specifications

Skill Level: Intermediate
Runner Size: 14 3/8" x 48 5/8"
Chair Pad: 16" x 18"
Chair Back: 16" x 22"
Toaster Cover: 12" x 10" x 6"
Block Size: 8" x 8"
Number of Blocks: 4

Apple
8" x 8" Block

Materials

- 1/4 yard red print for apples
- 1/3 yard light beige print for apple background
- Scraps green and brown prints
- Scraps red and light brown prints to cut 259 red and 248 light brown squares 2 1/2" x 2 1/2"
- 2 1/2 yards batting
- All-purpose thread to match fabrics
- Off-white quilting thread
- 14 1/2 yards red 1/2"-wide bias tape
- 1 oblong wooden bead for toaster cover handle
- 4 1/2 yards 1/4" cord
- Basic sewing supplies and tools

Rosy Red Apple Chair Pad
Placement Diagram
16" x 18"

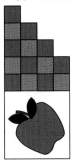

Making Apple Blocks

Step 1. Cut four squares light beige print 8 1/2" x 8 1/2".

Step 2. Prepare templates for apple pieces using full-size patterns given. Cut as directed on each piece, adding a 1/4" seam allowance to each piece when cutting for hand appliqué.

Step 3. Appliqué apple motifs on two 8 1/2" x 8 1/2" light beige print squares on the diagonal as shown in Figure 1 and in numerical order as indicated on full-size pattern. Appliqué the remaining apple motifs on the remaining two beige print squares with design centered on the squares as shown in Figure 2.

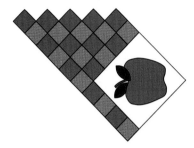

Figure 4
Sew a section to the top side of 1 diagonal Apple block as shown.

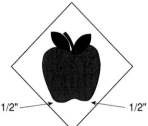

Figure 1
Appliqué apple motifs on the diagonal as shown.

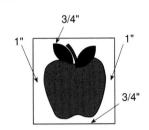

Figure 2
Appliqué apple motifs centered on square as shown.

Step 4. Press appliquéd blocks and set aside.

Table Runner

Step 1. Join five 2 1/2" x 2 1/2" squares alternating colors beginning with red; repeat for two rows. Join four 2 1/2" x 2 1/2" squares alternating colors beginning with red; repeat for two rows. Join three 2 1/2" x 2 1/2" squares alternating colors beginning with red; repeat for two rows. Join two 2 1/2" x 2 1/2" squares; repeat. Press seams in one direction.

Step 2. Join one strip of each row to make a section as shown in Figure 3; repeat for two sections. Press seams in one direction.

Figure 3
Join 1 strip of each row to make a section as shown.

Step 3. Sew a section to the top side of one diagonal Apple block as shown in Figure 4; repeat for second block. Press seams toward pieced sections.

Step 4. Join ten 2 1/2" x 2 1/2" squares alternating colors; repeat for second strip. Press seams in one direction. Sew a strip to the adjacent side of an already-stitched Apple block as shown in Figure 5; repeat with second block. Press seams toward strips.

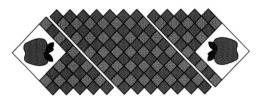

Figure 5
Sew a strip to the adjacent side of an already-stitched Apple block.

Step 5. Join eleven 2 1/2" x 2 1/2" squares alternating colors and beginning and ending with red; repeat for seven strips. Press seams in one direction.

Step 6. Join the two Apple sections with the 11-unit strips referring to Figure 6; press seams in one direction.

Figure 6
Join the 2 Apple sections with the 11-unit strips.

Step 7. Lay pieced top on a flat surface. Trim both side edges even with raw edge of end squares as shown in Figure 7.

Figure 7
Trim both side edges even with raw edge of end squares.

Step 8. Cut two pieces each 8 1/4" and 8 3/4" red bias tape. Cover seams between Apple blocks and squares, butting ends of bias tape as shown in Figure 8; hand-stitch both sides of bias tape in place.

Figure 8
Cover seams between blocks and
squares, butting ends of bias tape.

Step 9. Prepare table runner for quilting and finish with self-made or prepared red bias tape to finish. **Note:** *All projects were hand-quilted 1/4" away from apple motifs and in the ditch of diagonal seams of pieced squares using off-white quilting thread.*

Chair Back Pad

Step 1. Join four 2 1/2" x 2 1/2" squares, alternating colors; repeat for four pieced strips. Join two strips alternating beginning colors as shown in Figure 9; repeat. Press seams in one direction.

Figure 9
Join 2 strips as shown.

Figure 10
Sew a pieced strip to opposite
sides of 1 Apple block.

Step 2. Sew a pieced strip to opposite sides of one Apple block as shown in Figure 10; press seams toward strips.

Step 3. Join eight 2 1/2" x 2 1/2" squares, alternating colors; repeat for six strips. Join three strips, alternating beginning colors; repeat. Press seams in one direction.

Step 4. Sew a pieced strip to the top and bottom of the block/pieced section; press seams in one direction away from block.

Step 5. Cut red bias tape pieces and appliqué in place on Apple block as in Step 8 for table runner.

Step 6. Prepare for quilting and quilt as for table runner. Round corners using a plate or other round object.

Step 7. Cover 2 1/2 yards of 1/4" cord with red bias tape to make piping. Sew piping around outside edges of quilted chair back pad referring to the General Instructions.

Step 8. Join eight 2 1/2" x 2 1/2" squares, alternating colors; repeat for 11 strips. Join the strips, alternating beginning colors to make backing. Press seams in one direction.

Step 9. Cut four pieces red bias tape 13" long for ties. Pin ties to top of chair pad approximately 1 1/2" from corners as shown in Figure 11; stitch in place to secure.

1 1/2"

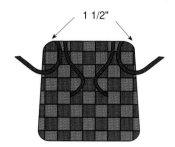

Figure 11
Pin ties to top of chair pad
approximately 1 1/2" from
corners as shown.

Step 10. Cut a second piece of batting 17" x 23". Layer with pieced backing and place right sides together with completed front. Stitch around all sides on piping seam line, leaving an 8" opening on one side. Trim batting and turn right side out; hand-stitch opening closed.

Chair Pad

Step 1. Join nine 2 1/2" x 2 1/2" squares, alternating colors; repeat for eight strips. Join the strips, alternating beginning colors to make chair pad top. Press seams in one direction. Repeat for chair pad backing.

Step 2. Finish chair pad as for chair back pad Steps 6 and 7 and 9 and 10, rounding back corners a little more than the front to fit chair seat and cutting batting 17" x 19".

Toaster Cover

Step 1. Join four 2 1/2" x 2 1/2" squares alternating colors; repeat for a second strip. Press seams in one direction. Sew to opposites sides of the remaining Apple block as shown in Figure 12; press seams toward strips.

Figure 12
Sew strips to Apple block as shown.

Step 2. Join six 2 1/2" x 2 1/2" squares alternating colors; press seams in one direction. Sew to the top of the pieced section again referring to Figure 12; press seams toward strips. Cut front piece top corners using Toaster Corner pattern given (page 81).

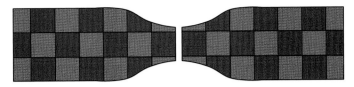

Step 3. Cut red bias tape and appliqué in place on three sides of the Apple block as in Step 8 for table runner.

Step 4. Join six 2 1/2" x 2 1/2" squares alternating colors; repeat for five strips, alternating beginning colors. Press seams in one direction. Join strips, alternating beginning colors, to make back piece. Press seams in one direction. Cut back piece top corners using Toaster Corner pattern given (see page 81).

Step 5. Join seven 2 1/2" x 2 1/2" squares alternating colors; press seams in one direction; repeat for six strips. Join three strips; press seams in one direction. Repeat for a second section. Using pattern given for side piece, cut as directed on the piece from the pieced strips as shown in Figure 13.

Figure 13
Cut side pieces from pieced sections as shown.

Step 6. Join the two side pieces at the center seam to make one long side piece as shown in Figure 14.

Figure 14
Join the 2 side pieces at the center seam to make 1 long side piece.

Step 7. Cut a 3" length of red bias tape for oblong wooden bead; slip on bead. Pin bias tape at edges on center right side of side piece as shown in Figure 15. *Note: The bias tape will not lie flat.*

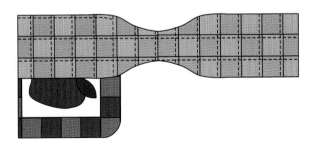

Figure 15
Pin bias tape at center on right side edges of side piece.

Step 8. Cut batting and lining pieces for toaster cover front and back using pieced sections as a pattern. Cut side using pattern piece given, placing seam line on pattern on fold of batting to eliminate seams in batting and lining.

Step 9. Pin batting pieces to the wrong side of pieced outside cover sections; pin lining pieces to batting side.

Step 10. Pin layered cover front to layered side piece with wrong sides together; stitch along seam as shown in Figure 16; repeat with layered back piece on remaining side of side piece.

Figure 16
Sew toaster cover front to side piece.

Step 11. Cut two 32" pieces red bias tape. Bind both curved edges of toaster cover. Cut a 38" piece red bias tape; bind bottom edge of toaster cover, overlapping beginning and end. ◩

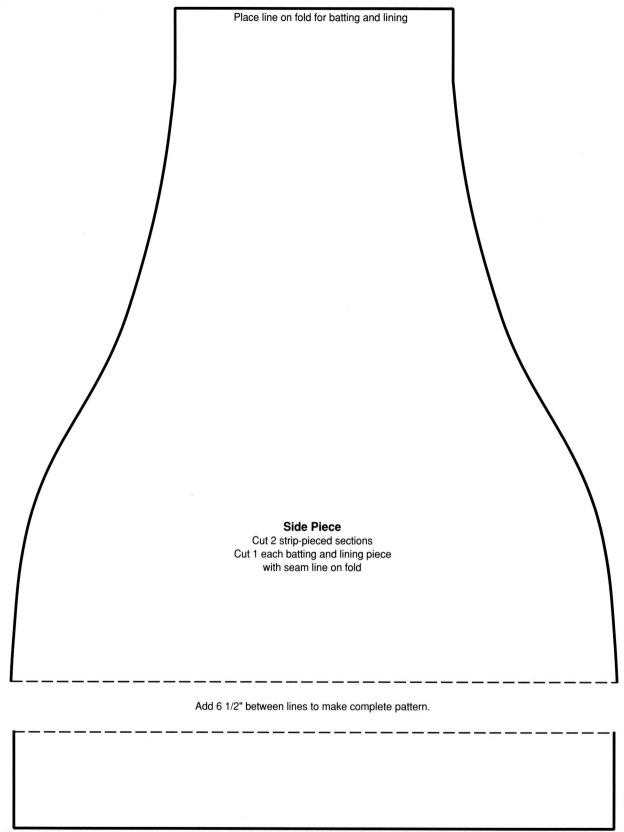

Place line on fold for batting and lining

Side Piece
Cut 2 strip-pieced sections
Cut 1 each batting and lining piece
with seam line on fold

Add 6 1/2" between lines to make complete pattern.

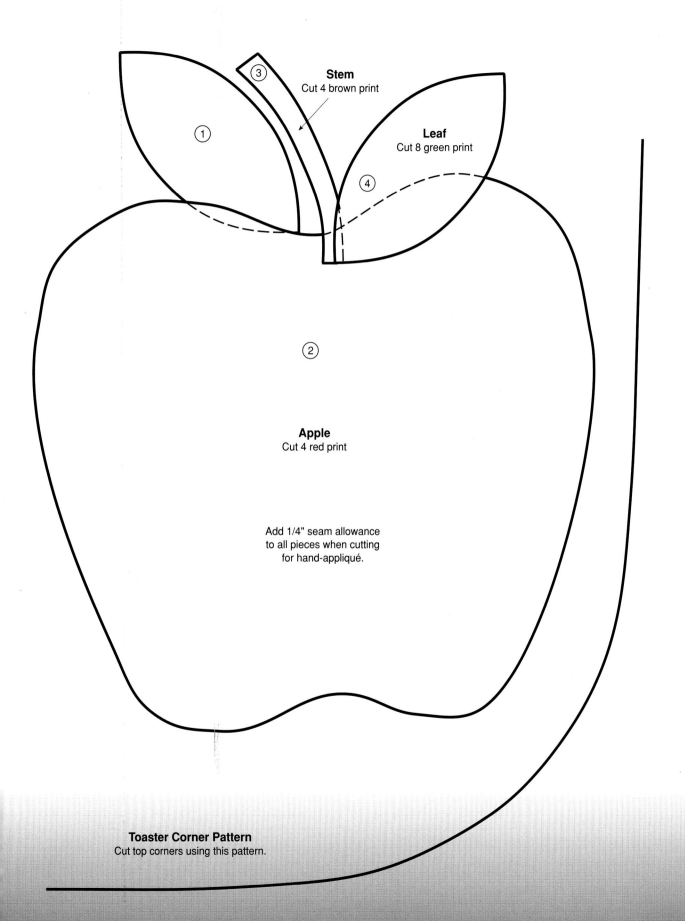

③

Stem
Cut 4 brown print

①

Leaf
Cut 8 green print

④

②

Apple
Cut 4 red print

Add 1/4" seam allowance
to all pieces when cutting
for hand-appliqué.

Toaster Corner Pattern
Cut top corners using this pattern.

Home Sweet Home

By Janice Loewenthal

Dig out those plaid and print scraps to make this homey-looking place mat set.

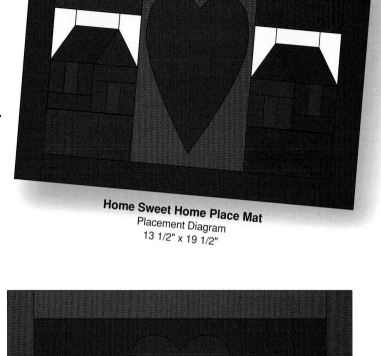

Home Sweet Home Place Mat
Placement Diagram
13 1/2" x 19 1/2"

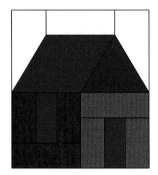

House Reversed
5" x 5 1/2" Block

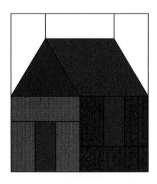

House
5" x 5 1/2" Block

Happy Home Place Mat
Placement Diagram
13 1/2" x 19 1/2"

Home Sweet Home Place Mat

Project Specifications
Skill Level: Intermediate
Project Size: 13 1/2" x 19 1/2"
Block Size: 5" x 5 1/2"
Number of Blocks: 2

Materials
- Assorted cream, gold, blue and green print/plaid scraps
- 7" x 11" rectangle tan print for background
- 7" x 10" rectangle burgundy print
- 1/4 yard burgundy/tan check
- Backing 12" x 18"
- Batting 12" x 18"
- Black and neutral color all-purpose thread
- Clear nylon monofilament
- 1/4 yard fusible transfer web
- Basic sewing supplies and tools

Instructions
Step 1. Wash and press all fabric scraps. Prepare templates using pattern pieces given. Cut as directed on each piece to make one House block.

Step 2. Sew B to C to B; repeat for two units. Sew an A piece to one long side of each pieced unit. Join the two pieced units to complete house bottom as shown in Figure 1.

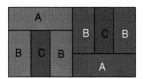
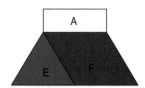

Figure 1
Join A-B-C units to
complete house bottom.

Step 3. Sew E to F and add A as shown in Figure 2. Sew D and DR to angled sides to complete roof unit as shown in Figure 3.

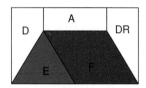

Figure 2
Sew E to F and add A.

Figure 3
Sew D and DR to the E-F-A
unit to complete roof unit.

Step 4. Join the house bottom with the roof unit to complete one House block; repeat for two identical blocks in one fabric selection, reversing F pieces to make a reverse block as shown in Figure 4.

Figure 4
Make 2 identical blocks,
reversing 1 block as shown.

Step 5. Cut four same-scrap rectangles 3" x 5 1/2". Sew a rectangle to the top and bottom of each pieced block; press seams toward rectangles.

Step 6. Trace the heart pattern onto the paper side of the fusible transfer web. Cut out shape leaving a margin all around. Fuse to the wrong side of the 7" x 10" burgundy print rectangle. Cut out on traced lines; remove paper backing.

Step 7. Center and fuse heart shape to the 7" x 11" tan print rectangle.

Step 8. Sew the appliquéd tan print rectangle between the two pieced block units as shown in Figure 5; press seams toward the rectangle.

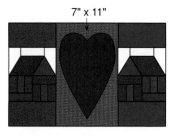

Figure 5
Sew the appliquéd rectangle
between 2 block units.

Step 9. Center pieced top on batting as shown in Figure 6; pin or baste layers together.

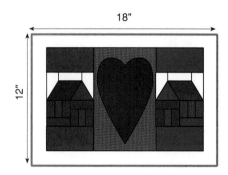

Figure 6
Center pieced top on 12" x 18"
batting piece as shown.

Step 10. Machine-appliqué heart shape in place using a machine zigzag or buttonhole stitch and black all-purpose thread in the top of the machine and bobbin.

Step 11. Place backing piece behind the batting layer with wrong side against batting. Machine-quilt in the ditch of seams and as desired using clear nylon monofilament in the top of the machine and neutral color all-purpose thread in the bobbin. Trim threads and excess batting and backing even with top.

Step 12. Cut four strips burgundy/tan check 3 1/2" x 17". Fold each strip in half along length with wrong sides together; press to form a crease. Unfold; sew one raw edge to each long side of quilted center as shown in Figure 7; fold to backside along crease line. Turn under long edge 1/4"; hand-stitch in place on backside.

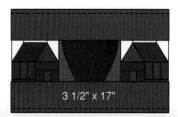

Figure 7
Sew 1 raw edge of strips to
each long side of quilted center.

Step 13. Sew the remaining burgundy/tan check strips to each short end as in Step 12, except center strip on sides with even excess at each end. Stitch as in Step 12; turn under long edge 1/4". Turn to backside, folding excess at each end to backside. Trim excess and fold at an angle on backside corners as shown in Figure 8; hand-stitch in place to finish.

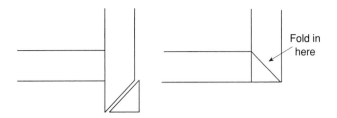

Figure 8
Trim excess and fold at an angle on backside corners.

Happy Home Place Mat

Project Specifications

Skill Level: Intermediate

Project Size: 13 1/2" x 19 1/2"

Block Size: 5" x 5 1/2"

Number of Blocks: 2

Materials

- Assorted cream, gold, blue and green print/plaid scraps
- 6" x 7" rectangle burgundy print
- 1/4 yard burgundy/tan check
- 1/4 yard tan print
- Backing 12" x 18"
- Batting 12" x 18"
- Black and neutral color all-purpose thread
- Clear nylon monofilament
- 1/8 yard fusible transfer web
- Basic sewing supplies and tools

Instructions

Step 1. Complete two identical House blocks with one reversed as in Steps 1–4 of Home Sweet Home Place Mat.

Step 2. Cut one rectangle dark print/plaid 3 1/4" x 6". Sew the rectangle between the two House blocks as shown in Figure 9; press seams toward rectangle.

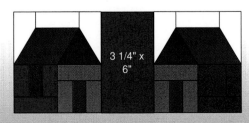

Figure 9
Sew the 3 1/4" x 6" rectangle between the 2 House blocks.

Step 3. Cut two strips burgundy/tan check 3" x 13 1/4".

Step 4. Cut and prepare the two heart pieces referring to Step 6 of Home Sweet Home Place Mat. Center and fuse the heart pieces to the strips cut in Step 3 as shown in Figure 10.

3" x 13 1/4"

Figure 10
Center and fuse the heart pieces to the strips.

Step 5. Sew a fused strip to the top and bottom of the pieced center section; press seams toward strips.

Step 6. Cut two strips burgundy/tan check 2 3/8" x 11". Sew a strip to each end of the pieced section; press seams toward strips.

Step 7. Appliqué heart pieces in place using black all-purpose thread and machine-quilt as in Steps 9–11 of Home Sweet Home Place Mat.

Step 8. Cut four strips tan print 3 1/2" x 17". Complete place mat referring to Steps 12 and 13 of Home Sweet Home Place Mat. ◼

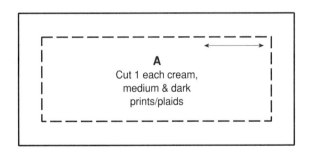

A
Cut 1 each cream, medium & dark prints/plaids

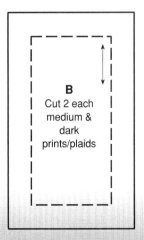

B
Cut 2 each medium & dark prints/plaids

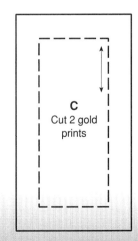

C
Cut 2 gold prints

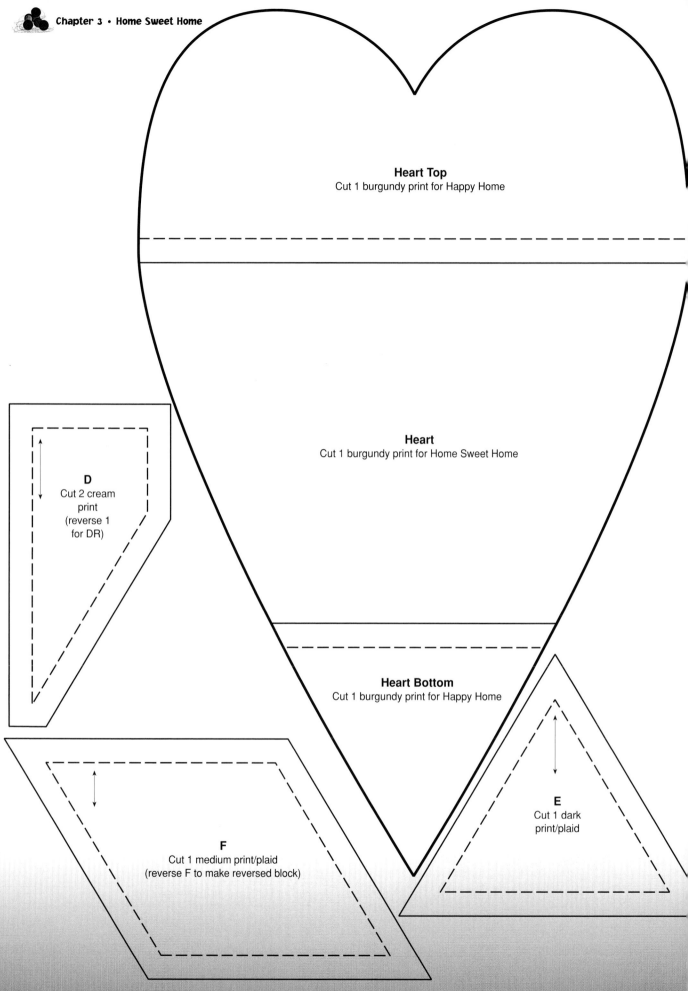

Heart Top
Cut 1 burgundy print for Happy Home

Heart
Cut 1 burgundy print for Home Sweet Home

D
Cut 2 cream
print
(reverse 1
for DR)

Heart Bottom
Cut 1 burgundy print for Happy Home

E
Cut 1 dark
print/plaid

F
Cut 1 medium print/plaid
(reverse F to make reversed block)

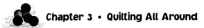

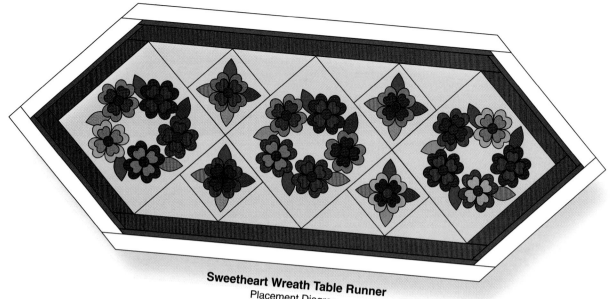

Sweetheart Wreath Table Runner
Placement Diagram
Approximately 21 1/2" x 57 1/2"

Sweetheart Wreath Table Runner and Coasters

Sweetheart Wreath Coaster
Placement Diagram
3 1/2" Diameter

By Norma Storm

Use scraps of coordinating red and green solids to create this hand-appliquéd table runner. If you prefer machine appliqué, you may create your version using those methods, but nothing compares to good hand-appliqué in quality.

Project Note
Each flower motif uses a lighter and darker shade of red solid. Refer to the project photo for color suggestions when choosing your fabric scraps.

Project Specifications
Skill Level: Intermediate
Table Runner Size: Approximately 21 1/2" x 57 1/2"
Coaster Size: 3 1/2" diameter
Block Size: 6" x 6" and 12" x 12"
Number of Blocks: 4 small and 3 large

Materials
- 1/8 dark green solid for border
- 1/4 yard total green solid scraps
- 1/4 yard coordinating dark red print or solid for border
- 3/4 yard total coordinating red solid scraps in a variety of shades
- 1 1/4 yards white-on-white print
- Backing 25" x 62"
- Batting 25" x 62"
- All-purpose thread to match fabrics
- Off-white quilting thread
- Basic sewing supplies and tools and fade-out pen

Table Runner
Step 1. Cut four 6 1/2" x 6 1/2" and three 12 1/2" x 12 1/2" squares white-on-white print.

Step 2. Prepare appliqué patterns using pattern pieces

given. Cut and prepare for appliqué referring to Hand-Appliqué instructions in the General Instructions, preparing five motifs for each large block and one for each small block.

Step 3. For large blocks, trace the circle pattern in the center of each 12 1/2" x 12 1/2" white-on-white print background block using fade-out pen.

Step 4. Using thread to match fabrics, hand-appliqué five motifs on each large square, referring to Figure 1 for order of appliqué and positioning for each motif.

Figure 1
Appliqué shapes in numerical order; appliqué each flower motif in the same order.

Step 5. Appliqué one motif in the center of each 6 1/2" x 6 1/2" white-on-white print background squares referring to Figure 2 for order of appliqué.

Figure 2
Appliqué shapes in numerical order.

Step 6. Cut two squares white-on-white print 9 3/4" x 9 3/4". Cut each square in half on both diagonals to make side fill-in triangles.

Step 7. Sew a triangle to two adjacent sides of a 6 1/2" x 6 1/2" block as shown in Figure 3; repeat for four block units; press seams toward triangles.

Figure 3
Sew a triangle to 2 adjacent sides of a small block.

Step 8. Arrange blocks as shown in Figure 4; join as shown to complete three sections. Join sections to complete the pieced center; press seams in one direction.

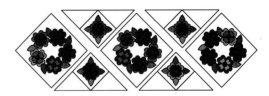

Figure 4
Arrange blocks as shown.

Step 9. Cut two strips dark red print or solid 1 1/2" x 37 1/2" and four strips 1 1/2" x 15 1/2". Sew a shorter strip to one side of one end, leaving 1 1/2" extending on each end as shown in Figure 5; press seam toward strip. Trim point end even with block as shown in Figure 6; repeat on opposite end.

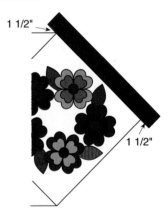

Figure 5
Leave 1 1/2" extending on each end.

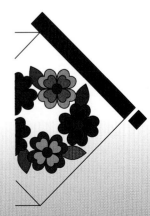

Figure 6
Trim point end even with block.

Step 10. Sew another short strip to the adjacent side of the runner end; press seam toward strip. Trim one end even with first strip. Trim remaining end at an angle even with runner edge as shown in Figure 7; trim remaining end of first strip in same manner. Repeat on opposite end.

Figure 7
Sew another short strip to adjacent
side; trim end at an angle even
with runner edge as shown.

Step 11. Sew a longer strip to opposite long sides; press seams toward strips. Cut each end even with end border strips as shown in Figure 8.

Figure 8
Trim border strips even
with end strips as shown.

Step 12. Cut two strips dark green solid 3/4" x 40" and four strips 3/4" x 15 1/2". Sew to ends and sides of table runner top referring to Steps 9, 10 and 11.

Step 13. Cut two strips white-on-white print 1 1/2" x 42" and four strips 1 1/2" x 18". Sew to ends and sides of table runner top referring to Steps 9, 10 and 11. Press completed table runner top.

Step 14. Place table runner on batting piece with wrong side of runner on batting. Place backing piece right sides together on the completed top; pin layers together.

Step 15. Stitch around outside edges, leaving an 8" opening on one side; trim batting and backing even with seams of runner top. Turn right side out; hand-stitch opening closed.

Step 16. Quilt as desired by hand or machine. *Note: The table runner shown was hand-quilted in the ditch of seams and around appliqué motifs using off-white quilting thread.*

Coasters

Step 1. Prepare template for coaster circle; cut as directed on piece.

Step 2. Prepare four leaf and two large petal shapes for hand-appliqué.

Step 3. Center and hand-appliqué two leaves on each of two white-on-white print circles and two large petals on the two remaining white-on-white print circles.

Step 4. Place one batting circle under appliqué circle. Place a red solid circle right sides together with a petal appliqué/batting circle; sew around outside edges, leaving a 2" opening. Clip curves all around; turn right side out; hand-stitch opening closed. Press to make round edges. Repeat for four coasters, using green solid circles for leaf coasters and the remaining red solid circle for a second petal coaster. ◰

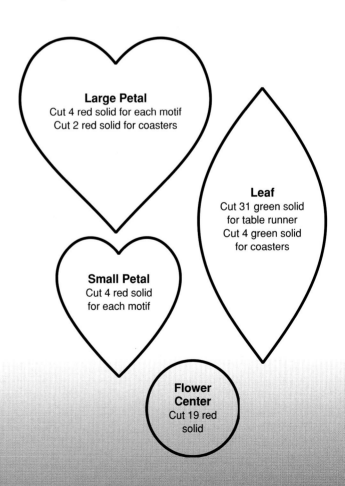

Large Petal
Cut 4 red solid for each motif
Cut 2 red solid for coasters

Leaf
Cut 31 green solid
for table runner
Cut 4 green solid
for coasters

Small Petal
Cut 4 red solid
for each motif

Flower Center
Cut 19 red solid

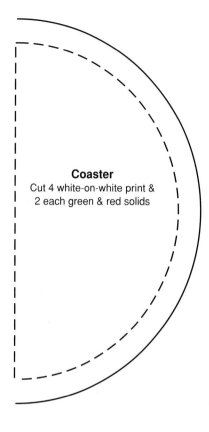

Coaster
Cut 4 white-on-white print &
2 each green & red solids

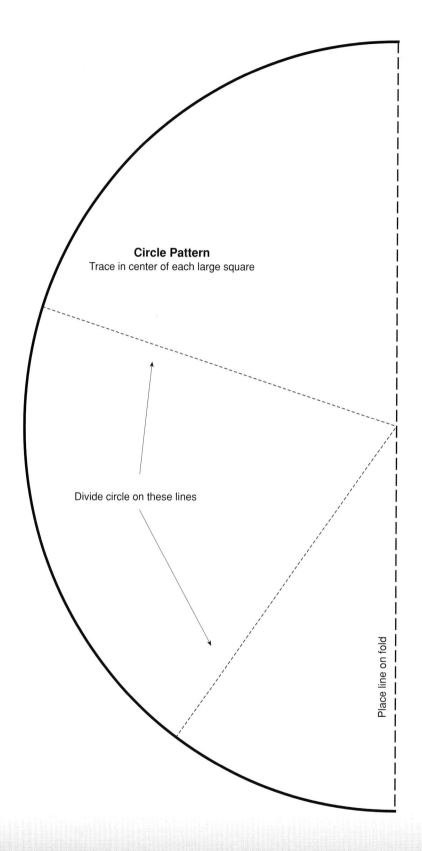

Circle Pattern
Trace in center of each large square

Divide circle on these lines

Place line on fold

Ladybug Table Set

By Beth Wheeler

Red, white and blue scraps combine to make this summery tablecloth with matching napkins. Eliminating the batting layer makes it possible to stitch up this pretty set in just a few hours.

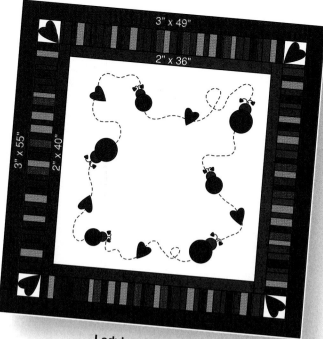

Ladybug Tablecloth
Placement Diagram
55" x 55"

Napkin
Placement Diagram
11 1/2" x 11 1/2"

Project Specifications

Skill Level: Beginner

Tablecloth Size: 55" x 55"

Napkin Size: 11 1/2" x 11 1/2"

Materials

- Scraps red, blue and red-and-blue prints
- 1 1/8 yards dark blue print
- 5/8 yard dark red print
- 1 1/8 yards white print
- 1 5/8 yards 60"-wide white solid or print for backing
- White all-purpose thread
- Red and blue rayon thread
- Blue pearl cotton
- 2/3 yard fusible transfer web
- Basic sewing supplies and tools, chalk pencil or fade-out pen

Instructions

Step 1. Cut a 36 1/2" x 36 1/2" square white print for center panel. Cut two strips each 2 1/2" x 36 1/2" and 2 1/2" x 40 1/2" dark blue print for inside borders.

Step 2. Sew the 2 1/2" x 36 1/2" dark blue print strips to opposite sides of the center panel; press seams toward strips. Sew the 2 1/2" x 40 1/2" dark blue print strips to the remaining sides; press seams toward strips.

Step 3. Cut red, blue and red-and-blue print scraps 6" long in varying widths from 1 1/2"–2 3/4". Join scrap pieces along 6" sides to form four strips at least 43" long referring to Figure 1. Trim each strip to 5" x 40 1/2" referring to Figure 2.

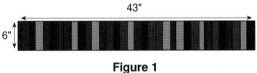

Figure 1
Join 6"-long by varying width scraps together along 6" sides to make a strip at least 6" x 43"

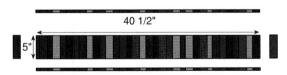

Figure 2
Trim strip to 5" x 40 1/2"

Step 4. Sew a 5" x 40 1/2" pieced strip to opposite sides of the center panel; press seams toward strips.

Step 5. Cut four squares white print 5" x 5". Sew a square to each end of the remaining 5" x 40 1/2" pieced strips. Sew these strips to remaining sides of the center panel; press seams toward strips.

Step 6. Cut and piece two strips each 3 1/2" x 49 1/2"

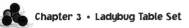

and 3 1/2" x 55 1/2" dark red print. Sew the shorter strips to two opposite sides and longer strips to remaining sides; press seams toward strips.

Step 7. Cut a 55 1/2" x 55 1/2" square from backing fabric. Lay on the pieced top with right sides together; stitch around outside edges leaving an 8" opening on one side. Turn right side out through opening; hand-stitch opening closed. Press completed pieced top.

Step 8. Prepare appliqué patterns using pattern pieces given. Trace shapes on the paper side of fusible transfer web referring to patterns for number to trace. Cut out shapes, leaving a margin all around.

Step 9. Fuse shapes to the wrong side of fabric scraps as directed on patterns for color. Cut out shapes on traced lines; remove paper backing.

Step 10. Draw a flight path on the center panel of the pieced top referring to the Placement Diagram and photo of project for positioning suggestions.

Step 11. Hand-stitch a long running stitch along marked line using blue pearl cotton; remove chalk pencil or fade-out pen marks.

Step 12. Arrange Ladybug bodies and heads and hearts on center panel referring to the Placement Diagram and photo of project for positioning suggestions. When satisfied with arrangement, fuse shapes in place referring to manufacturer's instructions.

Step 13. Mark antennae lines using chalk pencil or fade-out pen referring to patterns for shapes. Hand-stitch a running stitch along marked lines using blue pearl cotton; remove chalk pencil or fade-out pen marks. Fuse a small heart at the end of each antenna line. Fuse five medium hearts randomly along the embroidered flight path referring to the Placement Diagram for positioning suggestions. Fuse a large heart in each white print corner square.

Step 14. Machine satin-stitch around each fused shape using matching or contrasting rayon thread in the top of the machine and white all-purpose thread in the bobbin. Press well to finish.

Step 15. Cut four squares dark blue print 12 1/2" x 12 1/2". Turn under all edges 1/4"; press. Turn under again; stitch to hem edges.

Step 16. Using medium hearts cut in Steps 8 and 9, position and fuse one medium heart shape diagonally on one corner of each hemmed square; fuse in place.

Step 17. Using red rayon thread in the top of the machine and white all-purpose thread in the bobbin, machine satin-stitch around each heart shape to finish napkins. ◄

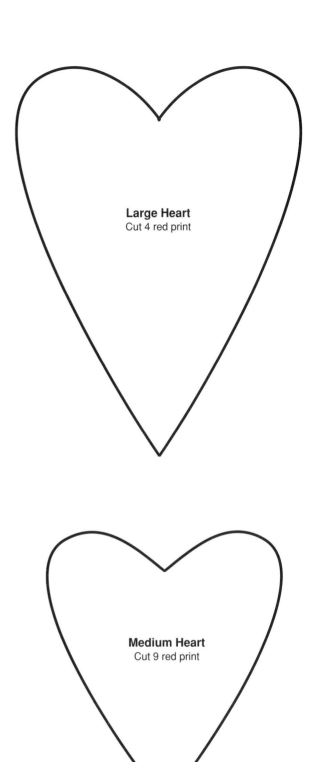

Large Heart
Cut 4 red print

Medium Heart
Cut 9 red print

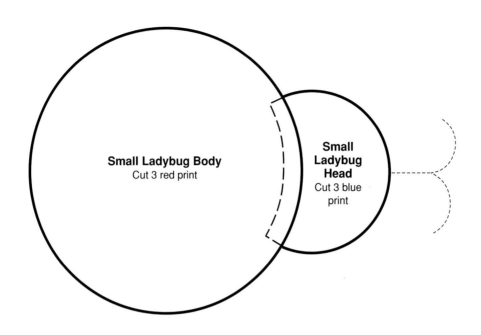

Small Ladybug Body
Cut 3 red print

Small Ladybug Head
Cut 3 blue print

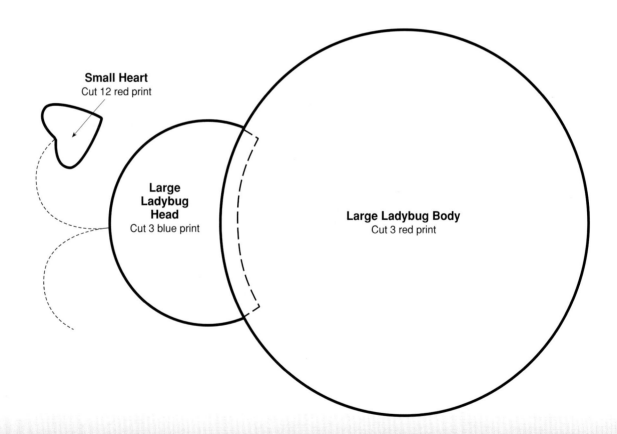

Small Heart
Cut 12 red print

Large Ladybug Head
Cut 3 blue print

Large Ladybug Body
Cut 3 red print

Americana Shirt, Skirt and Tote pattern begins on page 98

Chapter 4

Delightful Denim Duos

Denim is so popular with people of all ages that we've included an entire chapter of scrappy denim projects. Most of them use recycled jeans, but you can mix your old jeans with purchased denim if you need a few more shades to create a pleasing effect.

In This Chapter

Americana Shirt, Skirt and Tote

By Pearl Louise

If you like the scrappy Americana look, this outfit will be fashionable at the mall, a quilt show or even a country fair.

Scrappy Americana Shirt Front
Placement Diagram
Size Varies

Scrappy Americana
4" x 5" Block

Scrappy Americana
6 1/2" x 8 1/2" Block

Scrappy Americana Skirt
Placement Diagram
Size Varies

Shirt

Project Specifications

Skill Level: Beginner

Shirt Size: Size varies

Block Size: 4" x 5"

Number of Blocks: 4

Materials

- Adult-size denim shirt
- 3" x 18" scrap red print
- 8 scraps red print 1 1/2" x 3 1/2"
- 8 scraps blue print 1 1/2" x 4 1/2"
- 4 scraps beige print 2 1/2" x 3 1/2"
- 4 squares gold print 5" x 5"
- Neutral color all-purpose thread
- Gold 6-strand embroidery floss
- Basic sewing supplies and tools

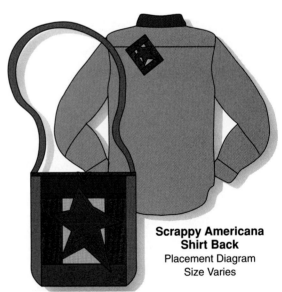

Scrappy Americana Shirt Back
Placement Diagram
Size Varies

Scrappy Americana Tote
Placement Diagram
6 1/2" x 8 1/2" x 3 1/4"

Instructions

Step 1. Wash all fabrics.

Step 2. Sew a 1 1/2" x 3 1/2" red print strip to the 3 1/2" sides of a beige print rectangle; press seams toward strips.

Sew a 1 1/2" x 4 1/2" blue print strip to the remaining sides of the stitched unit as shown in Figure 1; press seams toward strips.

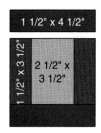

Figure 1
Sew a 1 1/2" x 4 1/2" blue print strip to the remaining sides of the stitched unit.

Step 3. Pin a small star shape on the stitched unit; sew around inside of each star 1/4" from outer edges of star to complete one block as shown in Figure 2. Repeat for four blocks.

Figure 2
Stitch 1/4" from edges of star shape.

Step 4. Arrange and pin two blocks on the right shirt front, one block on the left shirt front and one block on the top of the shirt left back shoulder referring to the Placement Diagram for positioning of blocks.

Step 5. Machine-stitch in the ditch of the seams of each beige print rectangle to attach blocks to shirt.

Step 6. Turn under outside edges of each block 1/4" and buttonhole-stitch in place using 2 strands gold embroidery floss as shown in Figure 3.

Figure 3
Turn under outside edges of each block 1/4" and buttonhole-stitch in place using 2 strands gold embroidery floss.

Step 7. To make the collar cover, fold the collar in half; place on a sheet of paper. Trace around the collar with a pencil to make pattern. Fold the 3" x 18" piece red print in half; pin collar pattern on folded fabric as shown in Figure 4 and cut out to make whole collar.

Figure 4
Pin collar pattern on folded fabric.

Step 8. Pin red print collar to shirt collar; buttonhole-stitch in place using 2 strands gold embroidery floss.

Step 9. Wash and dry the shirt to fray the edges of the star appliqués. Trim the frayed edges on each star and collar neatly.

Skirt

Project Specifications
Skill Level: Beginner
Skirt Size: Size varies—small, medium, large and extra large
Block Size: 6 1/2" x 8 1/2"
Number of Blocks: 20, 24, 28 or 32

Materials
- Scraps lightweight denim (old lightweight skirts, jumpers or shirts work best)
- Scraps red, blue, cream, tan and gold prints
- 1 yard 1"-wide elastic
- Basic sewing supplies and tools, safety pin and seam ripper

Instructions
Step 1. Wash all fabrics.

Step 2. Cut the following strips for each block: one 4" x 6" cream or tan print; two 2" x 6" red print; two 2" x 7" blue print; one star shape from gold print. Repeat for 20 blocks for small skirt, 24 blocks for medium skirt, 28 blocks for large skirt and 34 blocks for extra-large skirt.

Step 3. Sew a 2" x 6" red print strip to the 6" sides of the 4" x 6" cream or tan print rectangle; press seams toward strips. Sew the 2" x 7" blue print strips to the remaining sides; press seams toward strips.

Step 4. Pin a large star shape on the stitched unit; sew around inside of star 1/4" from outer edges of star to complete one block as shown in Figure 5. Repeat for number of blocks for chosen size skirt.

Figure 5
Pin a large star shape on the stitched unit; sew around star 1/4" from outer edges of star to complete 1 block.

Step 5. Cut 20 rectangles lightweight denim 7" x 9" (24, 28 or 32).

Step 6. Join five pieced blocks (six, seven or eight) with five lightweight denim squares (six, seven or eight) to make a row as shown in Figure 6; repeat for four rows. Join rows as shown in Figure 7 to make skirt bottom. Join skirt side edges to make a tube.

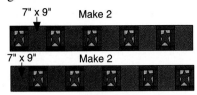

7" x 9"   Make 2
7" x 9"   Make 2

Figure 6
Join 5 pieced blocks with 5 denim
squares to make a row.

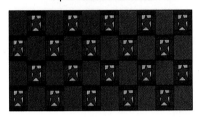

Figure 7
Join rows as shown.

Step 7. Cut enough 4"-wide strips from red print scrap fabrics to measure the length of the top edge of the skirt—65 1/2" for small, 78 1/2" for medium, 91 1/2" for large and 104 1/2" for extra large. Join strips on short ends to make one long strip; join ends to make a tube. Press the tube strip in half along length with wrong sides together to make waistband.

Step 8. Pin and sew the waistband to the skirt top edge using a 1/4" seam allowance and leaving a 2" opening to insert elastic.

Step 9. Put a safety pin on the end of the elastic. Insert through opening and pull through until the elastic comes back through the opening. Remove safety pin and adjust elastic to fit waist measurement; overlap ends of elastic and stitch together. Stitch several times to secure. Stitch remainder of waistband/skirt seam.

Step 10. Turn up bottom edge of skirt 1/2"; stitch to hem.

Step 11. Dampen the entire skirt with water. Lay the skirt flat and starting at the center, finger-gather skirt tightly. Twist the entire skirt tight and tie into a knot. Let the skirt air dry completely. Untwist and shake. Trim the frayed stars.

Tote

Project Specifications
Skill Level: Beginner
Tote Size: 6 1/2" x 8 1/2" x 3 1/4"
Block Size: 6 1/2" x 8 1/2"
Number of Blocks: 2

Materials
- Scraps lightweight denim
- Scraps red, blue, cream, tan and gold prints
- 1/4 yard red print for lining
- 1/4 yard lightweight batting
- Neutral color all-purpose thread
- 2 (3/4") blue buttons
- Basic sewing supplies and tools and toothbrush

Instructions
Step 1. Wash all fabrics. Make two 6 1/2" x 8 1/2" Scrappy Americana blocks referring to Steps 2–4 for Skirt.

Step 2. From lightweight denim scraps cut two 3 3/4" x 9" rectangles for tote sides, one 3 3/4" x 7" rectangle to tote bottom and 2 1/2"-wide strips to measure 42" when stitched together for strap.

Step 3. Sew the 2 1/2"-wide strips together on short ends to make strap.

Step 4. Join the two 3 3/4" x 9" side strips with the 3 3/4" x 7" bottom strip to make one long strip for sides and bottom as shown in Figure 8; press seams open.

3 3/4" x 9"   3 3/4" x 7"   3 3/4" x 9"

Figure 8
Join the two 3 3/4" x 9" side strips with
the 3 3/4" x 7" denim bottom strip to
make 1 long strip for sides and bottom.

Step 5. Sew the side/bottom strip to three sides of one pieced block as shown in Figure 9; repeat with other side of strip and second pieced block.

Figure 9
Sew the side/bottom strip to
3 sides of 1 pieced block.

Step 6. Cut the following from red print for lining and batting: two each 7" x 9" for front and back; two each 3 3/4" x 9" for sides; and one each 3 3/4" x 7" for bottom.

Step 7. Lay red print lining pieces right side up on corresponding size batting pieces; pin layers together to hold. Sew pieces together as in Steps 4 and 5.

Step 8. Insert bag lining inside bag with wrong sides together; pin.

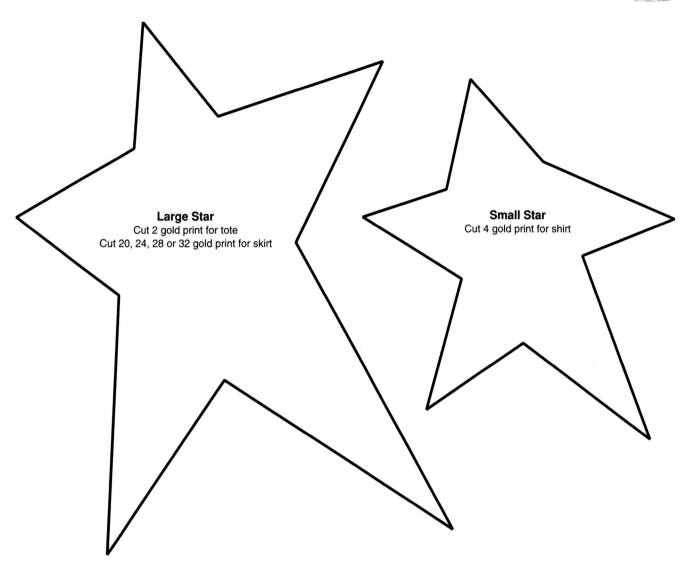

Large Star
Cut 2 gold print for tote
Cut 20, 24, 28 or 32 gold print for skirt

Small Star
Cut 4 gold print for shirt

Step 9. Fold one long edge of the 2 1/2" x 42" strap 1/2" to the wrong side; press. Lay the strip flat and fold the remaining raw edge under 1/4"; fold to cover the raw edge of the opposite edge as shown in Figure 10. Top-stitch down the center and 1/4" on each side of the center.

Figure 10
Lay the strip flat and
fold the pressed edge
over the raw edge.

Step 10. Place the strap inside the tote; sew the ends of the strap to the center top of each bag side as shown in Figure 11.

Step 11. Cut a 2" x 22" strip red print for binding. Fold strip along length with wrong sides together; press. Pin and sew raw edges to top edge of bag starting at the center

Figure 11
Sew the ends of the
strap to the inside center
top of each bag side.

front or back, overlapping ends. Turn folded edge to inside bag; hand-stitch in place. Fold strap up; hand-stitch strap piece to binding edge.

Step 12. Cut one piece red print 2" x 8". Fold the raw edges to the center; fold again and sew together to make closure loop.

Step 13. Fold the loop in half and sew a button to the raw ends on the center at the top of the tote back. Sew the remaining button to the top center of the tote front. Slip the folded loop over the button to close.

Step 14. Fray the star edges with a dampened toothbrush. ◻

Patch Happy Jumper

By Kathy Brown

Use any block to create a patch pocket to button to the front bib of a purchased jumper.

Four-Patch
8" x 8" Block

Nine-Patch
12" x 12" Block

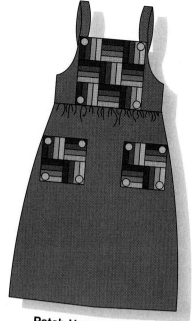

Patch Happy Jumper
Placement Diagram
Size Varies

Project Notes

Any block may be used to create pockets for a denim jumper. Use the instructions given to create Four-Patch and Nine-Patch blocks or choose your favorite blocks. Make several different block/pockets and change them as often as you like to add variety to your denim jumper.

Project Specifications

Skill Level: Beginner

Project Size: Size Varies

Block Size: 8" x 8" and 12" x 12"

Number of Blocks: 2 small, 1 large

Materials

- Purchased denim bib jumper
- 8 strips of fabric 1 1/2" x 36"
- 5/8 yard coordinating print
- 1 square 13" x 13" and 2 squares 9" x 9" lightweight batting
- 4 (1") wooden buttons
- 8 (7/8") wooden buttons
- All-purpose thread to match fabrics
- Basic sewing supplies and tools

Instructions

Step 1. Measure the bib portion of the purchased denim jumper to determine the size of the block needed to cover bib. *Note: The jumper shown is an adult size and uses one 12" x 12" block for bib and two 8" x 8" blocks for pockets.*

Step 2. Join four 1 1/2" x 36" strips with right sides together along length to make an A strip set ; press seams in one direction. Repeat with remaining four strips to make a B strip set. *Note: If a light strip is placed on one end of each strip set, a design is formed when piecing.*

Step 3. Cut each strip set into 4 1/2" segments as shown in Figure 1. You will need nine A and eight B segments.

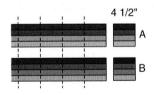

4 1/2"

Figure 1
Cut each strip set into 4 1/2" segments.

Step 4. Arrange four B segments with five A segments in three rows of three segments each as shown in Figure 2; join units in rows. Join rows to complete a Nine-Patch block for bib; press seams in one direction.

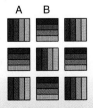

A   B

Figure 2
Arrange 4 B segments
with 5 A segments in 3
rows of 3 segments each.

Step 5. Arrange two B segments with two A segments to make a Four-Patch block as shown in Figure 3. Join segments in rows; join rows to complete one block. Press seams in one direction. Repeat for two Four-Patch blocks for pockets.

Figure 3
Arrange 2 B
segments with 2 A
segments to make a
Four-Patch block.

Step 6. Pin each block to a corresponding size batting piece with right side up. Quilt as desired by hand or machine. *Note: The blocks used on the sample jumper were machine-quilted in the ditch of seams joining segments.*

Step 7. Cut one 12 1/2" x 12 1/2" and two 8 1/2" x 8 1/2" squares coordinating print for lining. Place lining squares right sides together with corresponding blocks. Sew around all sides leaving a 3" opening on one side. Clip corners; turn right side out. Hand-stitch openings closed.

Step 8. Cut two 8" x 10 1/2" rectangles coordinating print for pocket backs. Turn under one 8" edge of each rectangle 1/2"; press. Turn under again 2"; stitch to make a hem.

Step 9. Place back pieces right sides together with quilted blocks. Stitch around three unhemmed sides as shown in Figure 4; clip corners. Turn right side out.

Figure 4
Sew around unhemmed sides.

Step 10. Topstitch 1/4" away from edges of each finished block/pocket.

Step 11. Make a buttonhole to fit 1" buttons 3/4" from each corner of the Nine-Patch block and a buttonhole to fit 7/8" buttons 3/4" from each corner of each Four-Patch block referring to Figure 5. *Note: If you don't care to remove these blocks to exchange for other blocks for a more versatile outfit, sew buttons and blocks directly on bib front and pocket areas.*

Buttonhole to fit 7/8" button

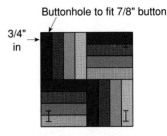

Buttonhole to fit 1" button

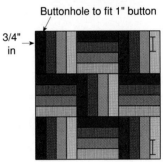

Figure 5
Make buttonholes 3/4"
in from each corner.

Step 12. Position block/pockets on jumper; pin. Mark placement of buttons on jumper. Hand-sew buttons on marked locations.

Step 13. Button the block/pockets onto the jumper to finish. ▪

Denim Bandanna Picnic Trio

By Marian Shenk

Denim and bandanna prints combine to make the perfect backyard barbecue apron, mitt and place mat set.

Denim Bandanna Mitt
Placement Diagram
Size Varies

Denim Bandanna Place Mat
Placement Diagram
14" x 20 1/2"

Project Notes

You may use bandanna handkerchiefs for patchwork, but it is less expensive to purchase bandanna fabric. Purchase a little extra and cut 14" x 14" squares for napkins. The edges may be fringed by pulling threads or hemmed to give a clean finish.

Project Specifications

Skill Level: Beginner
Apron Size: Size varies
Mitt Size: Size varies
Place Mat Size: 14" x 20 1/2"

Materials

- 1 3/4 yards blue denim
- 1/4 yard each red and blue bandanna prints
- 1 1/4 yards lightweight batting
- 10 yards self-made or purchased navy binding
- Navy or red and white all-purpose thread
- Purchased pattern for mitt and bib apron with pocket
- Basic sewing supplies and tools

Denim Bandanna Apron
Placement Diagram
Size Varies

Apron

Step 1. Cut commercial apron pattern pieces using blue denim.

Step 2. Cut a piece of batting using the apron pocket pattern. Lay on the wrong side of the denim pocket piece.

Step 3. Cut bandanna prints into large triangles and other shapes. Arrange cut shapes on the batting side of the layered pocket to entirely cover batting pieces; pin shapes in place. Using white all-purpose thread in the top of the machine and navy all-purpose thread in the bobbin, machine zigzag on edges of pieces to secure and finish edges. Trim any excess bandanna fabric even with pocket foundation.

Step 4. Stitch self-made or purchased navy binding to top edge of pocket referring to General Instructions.

Step 5. Pin finished pocket to bottom edge of apron; machine-baste in place along sides and bottom edges. Divide pocket into three equal sections. Stitch through all layers to secure sections.

Step 6. Make a V-yoke pattern to fit your apron referring to Figure 1; cut one batting piece using V-yoke pattern.

Step 7. Pin V-yoke batting piece to top of apron. Arrange and pin bandanna pieces cut in Step 3 to cover batting area referring to Figure 2 for shape suggestions and placement; stitch as in Step 3.

Figure 1
Make a V-yoke pattern to fit your apron as shown.

Figure 2
Arrange and pin bandanna pieces to cover batting area.

Step 8. Cut two pieces self-made or purchased binding to cover bottom edges of V-yoke section on apron front. Place one piece right sides together with stitched area as shown in Figure 3; stitch and press down. Repeat for second piece on opposite side; miter corner at center. Topstitch in place using navy all-purpose thread.

Figure 3
Place 1 piece right sides together with stitched area.

Step 9. Finish apron referring to the commercial pattern instructions, binding outside edges using self-made or purchased navy binding.

Mitt

Step 1. Cut commercial mitt pattern pieces using blue denim.

Step 2. Make a V-cuff pattern to fit the mitt referring to Figure 4; cut one batting piece using V-cuff pattern.

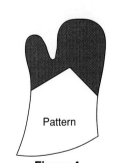

Pattern

Figure 4
Make a V-cuff pattern to fit your mitt as shown.

Step 3. Pin V-cuff batting piece to mitt top edge and cover with bandanna print shapes as in Step 3 for Apron.

Step 4. Bind bottom edges of V-cuff section as in Step 8 for Apron.

Step 5. Cut six batting pieces using mitt pattern. Sandwich blue denim mitt piece, three batting pieces and another blue denim mitt piece; machine-baste around edges. Repeat for second mitt unit. Layer stitched mitts

with V-cuff on top; machine-baste layers together.

Step 6. Bind all edges of mitt using self-made or purchased navy binding.

Place Mat

Step 1. Cut two pieces blue denim 14 1/2" x 21" for front and back and one piece 7" x 15" for pocket.

Step 2. Bind top edge of 7" x 15" pocket piece using self-made or purchased navy binding referring to the General Instructions.

Step 3. Center and pin bound pocket piece bottom to one 14 1/2" x 21" blue denim rectangle, matching raw edges; machine-baste in place around raw outside edges of pocket piece.

Step 4. Cut two pieces batting 3 1/2" x 14 1/2"; pin one piece to the right side of each end of the layered front/pocket piece as shown in Figure 5.

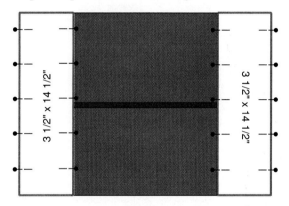

Figure 5
Pin 3 1/2" x 14 1/2" batting pieces to each end of the layered front/pocket piece.

Step 5. Cover each batting piece with bandanna print pieces and bind inside edge as in Steps 3 and 8 for Apron.

Step 6. Cut one piece batting 14 1/2" x 21". Sandwich between place mat front and remaining blue denim rectangle. Bind edges using self-made or purchased navy binding.

Step 7. Mark pocket area with a 9" pocket in the center as shown in Figure 6. Stitch through all layers to make pocket separations to place silverware, plate and napkin to finish. ■

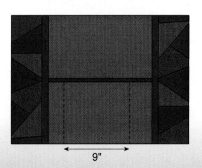

9"

Figure 6
Mark pocket area with a 9" pocket in the center as shown.

Zigzag Denim Exercise Mat and Duffel Bag

By Holly Daniels

If you're looking for a way to use up lots of scraps, this is the project for you. Maybe seeing bits of some of your favorite fabrics will inspire you to exercise more often.

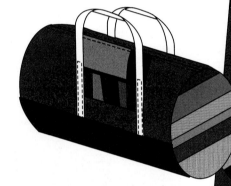

Zigzag Denim Duffel Bag
Placement Diagram
Approximately 8 1/2" x 25 1/2"

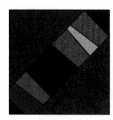

Zigzag
7" x 7" Block

Project Notes

Two denim skirts and three pairs of jeans plus other cotton print scraps were combined to create this exercise set. Exercise might help you lose weight and make scraps from the jeans you are now wearing to create future denim scrap projects.

Project Specifications

Skill Level: Intermediate

Exercise Mat Size: 28" x 56"

Duffel Size: Approximately 8 1/2" x 25 1/2"

Block Size: 7" x 7"

Number of Blocks: 32

Materials

- Variety of print scraps to total 1 1/2 yards
- Denim scraps to total 2 yards
- 1 yard lining fabric
- 1 yard muslin
- Backing 32" x 60"
- Batting 32" x 60"

Zigzag Denim Exercise Mat
Placement Diagram
28" x 56"

- 2 pieces each thin batting 10" x 10" and 15" x 26"
- 5 1/4 yards self-made or purchased binding
- Neutral color and white all-purpose thread
- Gold cotton thread
- 26"-long white sport zipper
- 60" piece 1"-wide white nylon webbing
- Basic sewing supplies and tools

Exercise Mat

Step 1. Cut scraps into 3"-long by varying widths rectangles.

Step 2. Cut 32 muslin rectangles 3" x 11".

Step 3. Using the flip-and-sew method (see General Instructions), cover each muslin piece with 3" scrap rectangles as shown in Figure 1.

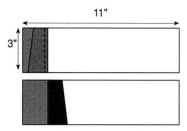

Figure 1
Use flip-and-sew method to
cover 3" x 11" rectangles with
3" scrap rectangles.

Step 4. Prepare template for piece A using pattern piece given. Trim ends of stitched 3" x 11" segments using A as shown in Figure 2.

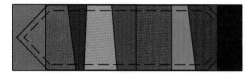

Figure 2
Trim using piece A.

Step 5. Cut 32 squares 6 1/8" x 6 1/8" from denim scraps. Cut each square in half on one diagonal to make B triangles. *Note: If denim scraps are too small to cut squares, prepare template for piece B; cut 64 B pieces from denim scraps.*

Step 6. Sew a B triangle to each long side of a pieced A as shown in Figure 3; press seams open to reduce bulk. Repeat for 32 blocks.

Figure 3
Sew B to each long side of A.

Step 7. Arrange blocks in eight rows of four blocks each referring to the Placement Diagram for positioning of blocks. Join blocks in rows; join rows to complete quilt top. Press seams open to reduce bulk.

Step 8. Prepare for quilting and finish referring to the General Instructions. *Note: The quilt shown was machine quilted using gold cotton thread in the top of the machine and all-purpose thread in the bobbin. The quilting is 1/4" from seams of all pieces as shown in Figure 4.*

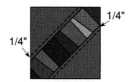

Figure 4
Machine-quilt 1/4"
from A piece seams.

Duffel Bag

Step 1. To make pockets, cut two rectangles muslin 3" x 7". Cut scrap fabrics and stitch to muslin rectangles as in Steps 1 and 3 for Exercise Mat.

Step 2. Cut two pieces denim 3 1/2" x 7". Sew a piece to one 7" side of each strip-pieced section to make pocket fronts as shown in Figure 5; press seams open.

Figure 5
Sew a 3 1/2" denim
piece to the 7" sides of
the pieced sections.

Step 3. Cut two pieces lining fabric 6" x 7". Layer one with each pocket with wrong sides together; baste around edges.

Step 4. Cut two pieces of denim 1 1/4" x 7". Fold under one long edge 1/4" on each piece; press. Pin remaining 7" raw edges of each piece to the strip-pieced 7" edge of layered pockets with right sides together; stitch. Turn denim strips to the lining side of the pockets; hand- or machine-stitch in place. Set aside.

Step 5. Cut two pieces lining 15" x 26". Place one piece of lining right side down on a flat surface; place 15" x 26" piece thin batting on top. Cut pieces of denim scraps at least 15 1/2" long. Sew denim pieces to lining/batting foundation using flip-and-sew method referring to the General Instructions to make bag side. Repeat for second lining and batting pieces. Trim excess even with lining piece.

Step 6. Topstitch 1/4" on each side of seams using gold cotton thread in the top of the machine and all-purpose thread in the bobbin.

Step 7. Center one pocket on one stitched bag side as shown in Figure 6.

Step 8. Cut two 30" pieces of 1"-wide white nylon webbing. Pin one piece of webbing to bag side covering raw edges of pocket as shown in Figure 7. Stitch in place using white all-purpose thread, again referring to Figure 7. Repeat for second bag side.

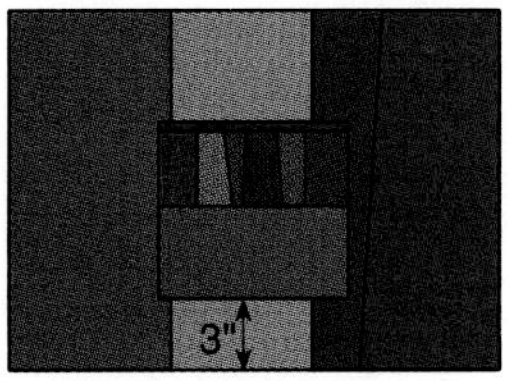

Figure 6
Center 1 pocket on
1 stitched bag side.

Figure 7
Pin 1 piece of webbing to bag
side covering raw edges of
pocket as shown; stitch in place.

Step 9. Cut two strips denim scrap 4" x 26". Pin one strip 3" from bottom of bag side along raw edge of pocket with right sides together as shown in Figure 8; stitch. Repeat for second bag side.

Figure 8
Pin 1 strip 3" from bottom of each
bag side along raw edge of pocket
with right sides together.

Step 10. Flip strips down to cover bottom; trim seam even with bottom edge of bag sides.

Step 11. Align white sport zipper edge with top edge of bag side with right sides together as shown in Figure 9. Sew close to zipper teeth using white all-purpose thread. Repeat on opposite side; press seams away from zipper.

Topstitch 1/4" from fabric edge as shown in Figure 10. *Note: If seam is too bulky, trim and finish zipper seam allowances with a zigzag stitch or overlock stitch.*

Figure 9
Align zipper edge with top
edge of bag side with right
sides together.

Figure 10
Topstitch 1/4" from fabric edge.

Step 12. Overlap loose ends of zipper; tack in place by hand as shown in Figure 11.

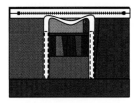

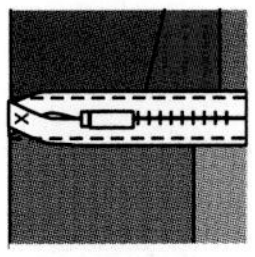

Figure 11
Overlap loose ends
of zipper; tack in
place by hand.

Step 13. Fold bag with right sides together; sew bottom seams using a 1/2" seam allowance.

Step 14. Cut two 10" x 10" squares muslin. Place a 10" x 10" piece thin batting on each piece. Using the flip-and-sew method, stitch print scraps to cover layered pieces. Trim to make a 9" circle from each square using circle pattern given.

Step 15. Sew a circle to each end of the bag to finish. *Note: Zigzag stitch or overlock stitched seams to prevent fraying, if desired.* 🔳

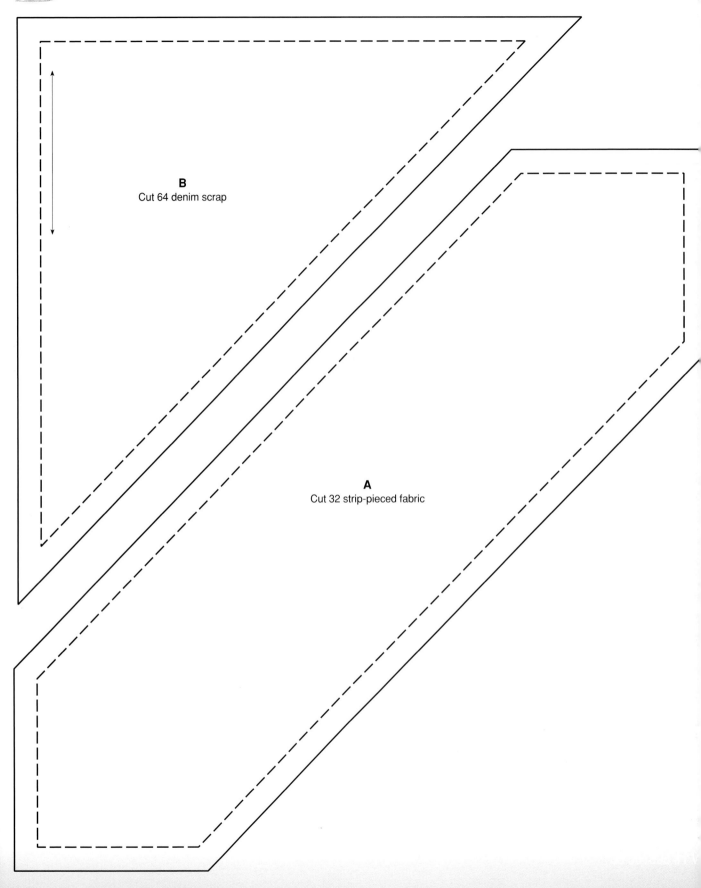

B
Cut 64 denim scrap

A
Cut 32 strip-pieced fabric

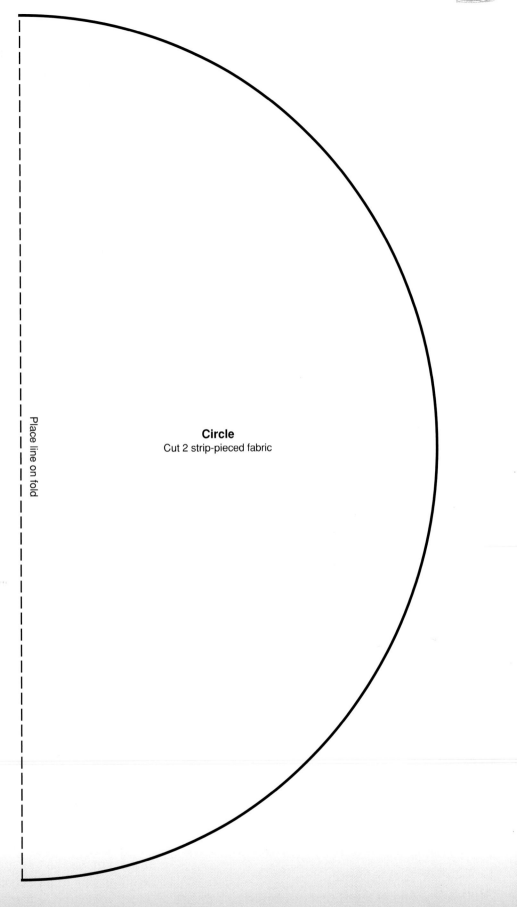

Circle
Cut 2 strip-pieced fabric

Place line on fold

Crazy-Patch and Plaid Christmas Stockings

By Patsy Moreland

Old and worn-out denim blue jeans are the perfect source for the crazy patchwork making up this sturdy Christmas stocking and stocking ornament.

Crazy-Patch and Plaid Stocking Placement Diagram
11" x 15 1/4"

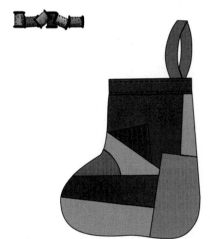

Crazy-Patch and Plaid Stocking Ornament
Placement Diagram
3 1/2" x 4 1/4"

Large Stocking

Project Specifications

Skill Level: Beginner

Stocking Size: 11" x 15 1/4"

Materials

- 3 pairs adult-size denim blue jeans (light, medium and dark colors); one with coin pocket
- 3 squares 18" x 18" prewashed muslin
- 1/8 yard tartan plaid
- White all-purpose thread
- Variegated metallic thread
- 1 package 1/4"-wide fusible transfer webbing strip
- Denim sewing-machine needle
- Basic sewing supplies and tools and seam ripper

Instructions

Step 1. Prepare pattern for large stocking using pattern given and referring to Figure 1. Cut as directed on pattern.

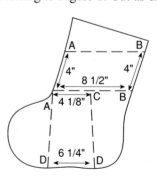

Figure 1
Combine stocking pieces,
adding inches between
letters as shown.

Step 2. Cut one pair of blue jeans from bottom of pant hem to above the knee. Cut along one leg seam to open outside flat seam on each pant leg as shown in Figure 2.

Step 3. Pin stocking pattern to one flat piece with top even with pant hem stitching as shown in Figure 3; cut out including pant hem on top of pattern.

Step 4. Cut out two muslin shapes using denim stocking piece as pattern.

Figure 2
Cut along 1 leg seam to open flat seam on each pant leg.

Figure 3
Pin stocking pattern to 1 flat piece with top even with pant hem stitching; cut out.

Step 5. Cut one piece from pants hem area 1" x 9" or 1/2" above hem stitching line.

Step 6. Cut the coin pocket from pants with 1/2" of denim fabric extending beyond pocket area.

Step 7. Cut three belt loops from denim waistband; use seam ripper to remove waistband fabric.

Step 8. Cut 26 denim patches as follows: 3" x 4"; 1 3/4" x 2 3/4"; and small 1" x 3 1/2".

Step 9. Cut a strip of 1/4"-wide fusible transfer webbing strip; place on wrong side of one denim shape on the raw edge; iron in place with paper side up. Remove paper; fold denim over fused strip. Press firmly with continuous steam for about 10 seconds. Fuse two edges of 14 denim pieces. Fuse one edge of 12 denim pieces. *Note: Either side of the denim may be used as the right side.*

Step 10. Cut 10 squares tartan plaid 2 1/2" x 2 1/2". Fold each square in half with wrong sides together. On folded edge, fold corners to bottom center as shown in Figure 4; press and pin.

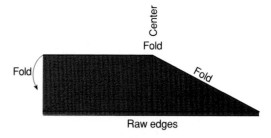

Figure 4
Fold each square in half with wrong sides together. Fold corners to bottom center.

Step 11. Pin coin pocket to one muslin stocking shape. Pin the folded and fused edge of one denim shape over the coin pocket extension as shown in Figure 5. With variegated metallic thread in the top of the machine and white all-purpose thread in the bobbin and the denim sewing-machine needle in place, topstitch 1/16" along folded denim edge. Pin another denim piece over stitched piece and stitch in place referring to Figure 6 for placement.

Figure 5
Pin the folded and pressed edge of 1 denim shape over the coin pocket extension.

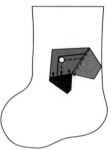

Figure 6
Pin another denim piece over stitched piece and stitch in place.

Step 12. Continue adding pieces in numerical order, placing a tartan point under folded edge of third piece and topstitch two sides of piece 3 and one side of piece 4 referring to Figure 7. Cover muslin with patches of denim, inserting tartan points as indicated in Figure 8.

Step 13. Press using pressing cloth; trim excess patches even with muslin foundation.

Step 14. Pin and sew the 1" x 9" pant hem strip with right sides together along top edge of finished stocking front; stitch in place using all-purpose thread.

Step 15. Pin the denim stocking shape right sides together with the finished stocking piece; stitch using a 1/2" seam allowance.

Step 16. Place two remaining muslin stocking shapes right sides together; stitch all around using a 1/2" seam allowance, leaving top edge open. Press under top edge 1/4".

Step 17. Insert muslin stocking inside denim stocking with wrong sides together. Using variegated metallic

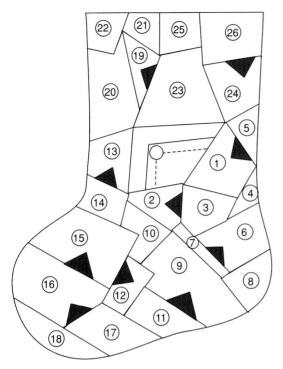

Figure 7
Continue adding pieces in numerical order, placing a tartan point under folded edge of third piece and topstitch 2 sides of piece 3 and 1 side of piece 4.

Figure 8
Cover muslin with patches of denim, inserting tartan points.

thread in the top of the machine and white all-purpose thread in the bobbin, stitch around top of stocking from the right side to stitch muslin lining in place.

Step 18. Join three belt loops on short ends, overlapping ends as shown in Figure 9. Topstitch over overlapped ends. Place ends of stitched loops on the stocking top 1/2" from side seams as shown in Figure 10. Topstitch around top of stocking two more times 1/8" from first stitching and 1/8" apart, stitching over belt loops to finish.

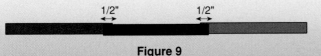

Figure 9
Join 3 belt loops on short ends, overlapping ends.

Figure 10
Place ends of stitched loops on the stocking top 1/2" from side seams.

Stocking Ornament

Project Specifications

Skill Level: Beginner

Project Size: 3 1/2" x 4 1/4"

Materials

- 5" x 5" square blue denim
- 2 denim blue jeans belt loops
- 7 squares 2 1/2" x 2 1/2" denim in a variety of shades
- 1 blue jeans pant hem piece 1" x 7"
- 2 squares 2" x 2" tartan plaid
- 5" x 5" square muslin
- White all-purpose thread
- Variegated metallic thread
- 1 package 1/4"-wide fusible transfer webbing strip
- Denim sewing-machine needle
- Basic sewing supplies and tools and seam ripper

Instructions

Step 1. Prepare pattern for stocking ornament using pattern given. Cut as directed on pattern.

Step 2. Remove waistband from belt loops using the seam ripper.

Step 3. Prepare edges of six 2 1/2" x 2 1/2" denim squares referring to Step 9 for Large Stocking, fusing over one edge of five squares and two edges of two squares.

Step 4. Fold and pin 2" x 2" tartan plaid squares as in Step 10 for Large Stocking.

Step 5. Pin and stitch denim shapes to one muslin stocking shape referring to Steps 11 and 12 for Large Stocking and Figure 11 using variegated metallic thread in the top

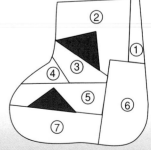

Figure 11
Pin and stitch pieces to muslin as shown.

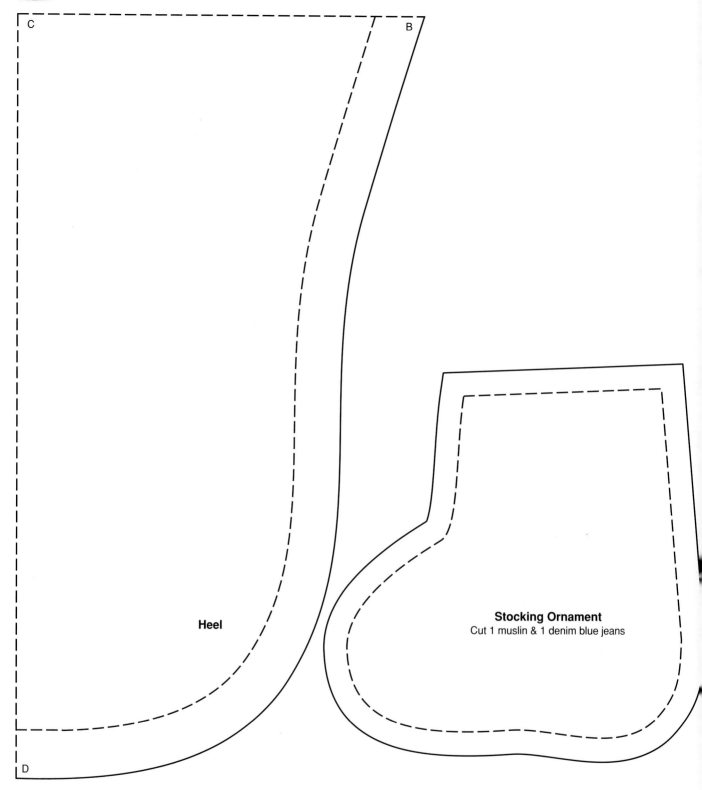

C

B

Heel

Stocking Ornament
Cut 1 muslin & 1 denim blue jeans

D

of the machine and white all-purpose thread in the bobbin.

Step 6. Cut the 1" x 7" pant hem piece in two 3 1/2" lengths. Pin and stitch one 1" x 3 1/2" pant hem piece to the top of the patched stocking with right sides together; trim excess.

Step 7. Pin and stitch the remaining 1" x 3 1/2" pant hem piece to the top of the denim stocking back; trim excess.

Step 8. Join the two belt loops on short ends. Pin to the top wrong side edge of stocking back; machine-baste in place.

Step 9. Pin the pieced stocking right sides together with the stocking back; stitch around sides with a 1/4" seam allowance, leaving top edge open. Turn right side out; topstitch two rows of stitching across stocking ornament top to finish. ⌧

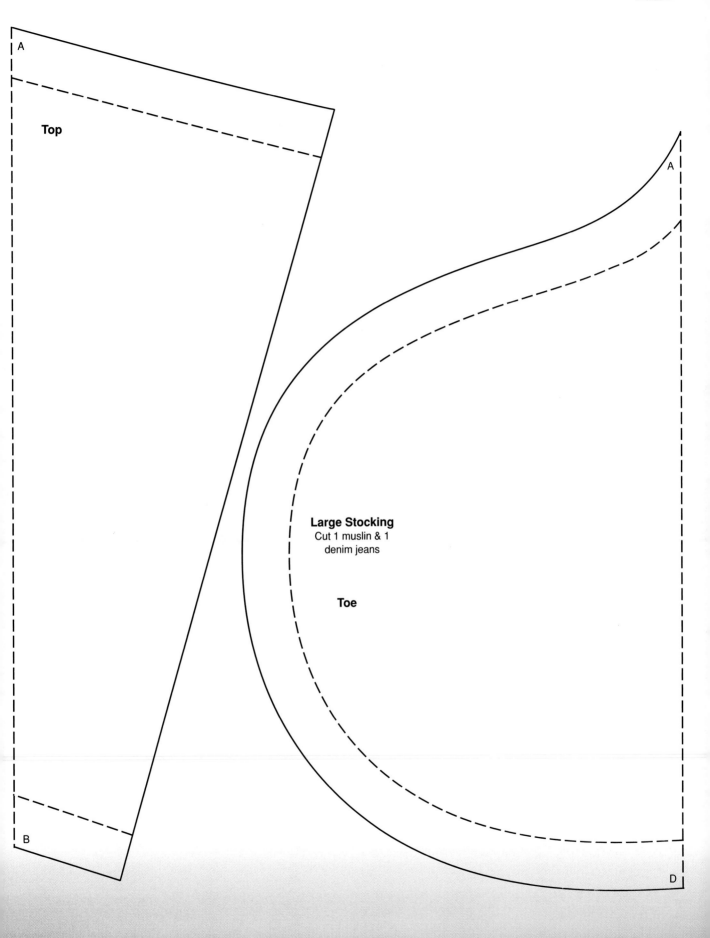

A

Top

A

Large Stocking
Cut 1 muslin & 1
denim jeans

Toe

B

D

Denim Doggie and Dorm Room Throw

By Beth Wheeler

Our snuggle-size quilt is perfect for a dorm-room throw or late-night TV nest. It's a thrifty way to recycle old blue jeans and small scraps left from other quilting projects.

Denim Dorm Room Throw
Placement Diagram
48" x 48"

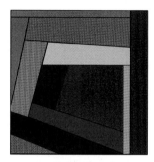

Denim Dorm Room
12" x 12" Block
(unfinished size)

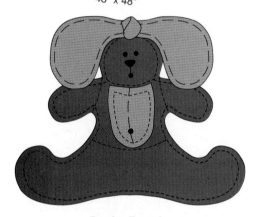

Denim Doggie
Placement Diagram
Approximately 8" x 11"

Denim Dorm Room Throw

Project Specifications

Skill Level: Beginner

Quilt Size: 48" x 48"

Block Size: 12" x 12"

Number of Blocks: 16

Materials

- 16 (12") muslin squares
- Scraps of denim from old blue jeans
- Large scraps pink and blue prints
- Backing 48" x 48"
- 5 1/2 yards self-made or purchased binding
- Neutral color all-purpose thread
- Navy rayon thread
- Fray preventative
- Basic sewing supplies and tools

Instructions

Step 1. Cut pink and blue print scraps into wedge-shaped strips 1" wider on one end than on the other end as shown in Figure 1.

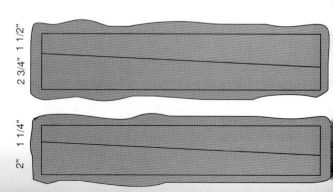

Figure 1
Cut fabric scraps into wedge shapes 1" wider on
1 end than on the other end.

Step 2. Prepare templates using pattern pieces given.

Step 3. Cut 16 assorted shapes from denim scraps using templates given. *Note: You may use pockets from old blue jeans instead of cut shapes, if desired.*

Step 4. Place a denim shape anywhere on one 12" x 12" muslin square. Strip-piece fabric wedges around the denim shape as shown in Figure 2. Continue adding shapes until the muslin square is covered. Press and trim any excess fabric even with muslin square edges. Repeat for 16 blocks.

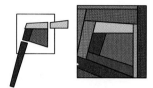

Figure 2
Strip-piece fabric wedges
around the denim shape.

Step 5. Using navy rayon thread in the top of the machine and all-purpose thread in the bobbin, add machine embroidery stitches around each shape.

Step 6. Arrange finished blocks on the 48" x 48" square backing with wrong sides together. The blocks should touch but not overlap. Stitch through all layers with a straight stitch close to all edges of each block.

Step 7. Cut 12 strips denim 1 1/4" x 12". Center strips over raw edges of blocks in each row referring to Figure 3; stitch close to raw edges of strips referring to Figure 4. Apply fray preventative to strip edges. *Note: Use pinking shears to cut strips if you prefer not to use fray preventative. The designer recommends using a fray preventative that prevents fraying without stiffness (see page 176).*

Figure 3
Place strips over raw edges
of blocks in each row.

Figure 4
Stitch close to raw
edges of strips.

Step 8. Cut three strips denim 1 1/4" x 48". Place strips over raw edges of blocks between rows; stitch close to raw edges of strips. Apply fray preventative to strip edges.

Step 9. Bind edges with self-made or purchased binding referring to the General Instructions.

Denim Doggie

Project Specifications
Skill Level: Beginner
Project Size: Approximately 8" x 11"

Materials
- Pair of old denim blue jeans
- Scrap pink-and-white plaid
- Black all-purpose thread
- Black pearl cotton or 6-strand embroidery floss
- 4 (1/4") black half-round buttons
- Weighting pellets
- Polyester fiberfill
- Basic sewing supplies and tools and pinking shears

Instructions
Step 1. Prepare templates using pattern pieces given. Transfer all marks to patterns pieces. Cut as directed on each shape, cutting ears and tummy using pinking shears.

Step 2. Using black pearl cotton or 6-strand embroidery floss, satin-stitch nose and straight-stitch mouth on body piece referring to marks on Face pattern.

Step 3. Using black pearl cotton or 6-strand embroidery floss and a running stitch, sew tummy piece to body piece referring to pattern for placement.

Step 4. Place ear pieces wrong sides together. Using black pearl cotton or 6-strand embroidery floss and a running stitch, sew ear pieces together. Tie ear pieces in a knot in the center.

Step 5. Place body pieces with wrong sides together; insert gusset matching dots on gusset with dots on body pattern. Machine-stitch 1/4" from edges all around using black all-purpose thread, leaving an opening on the top of the head as marked on pattern. Stitch again 1/8" away from first stitching to reinforce seam.

Step 6. Fill arms and legs with weighting pellets so limbs are squishy, not firm. Machine-stitch across arms and legs as marked on pattern.

Step 7. Fill body area with weighting pellets until squishy; machine-stitch across neckline as marked on pattern.

Step 8. Stuff head with polyester fiberfill; hand-stitch opening in head closed.

Step 9. Stitch ears to doggie's head under knot area. Sew black half-round buttons in place for eyes, mouth and belly button as marked with X's on pattern and as shown on Face Pattern to finish. ◾

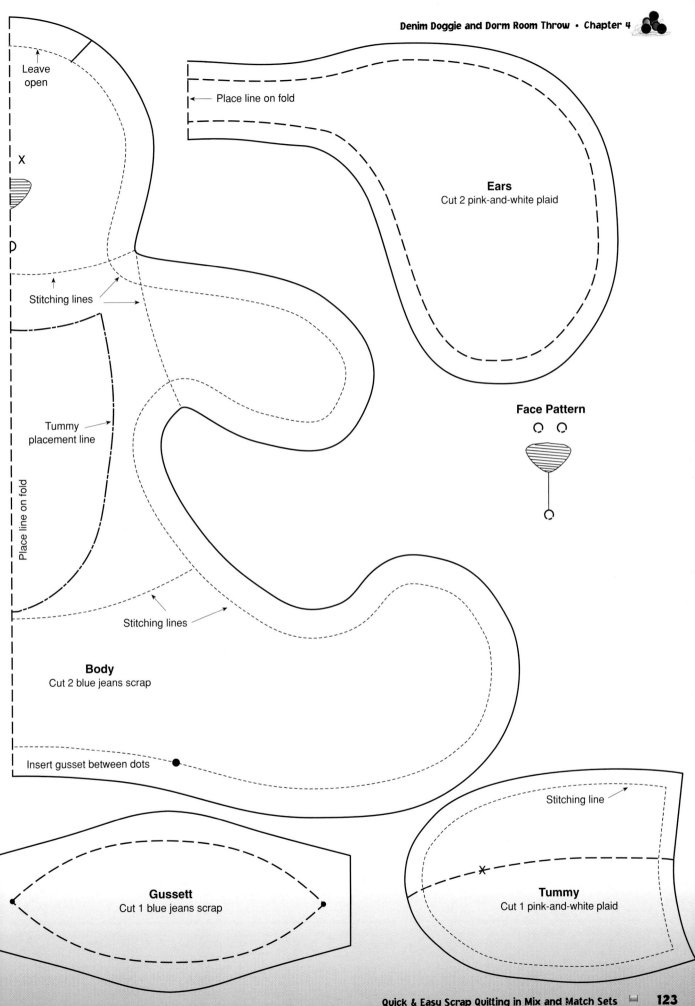

Leave open

X

D

Stitching lines

Place line on fold →

Ears
Cut 2 pink-and-white plaid

Face Pattern

Tummy placement line

Place line on fold

Stitching lines

Body
Cut 2 blue jeans scrap

Insert gusset between dots

Stitching line

Gussett
Cut 1 blue jeans scrap

Tummy
Cut 1 pink-and-white plaid

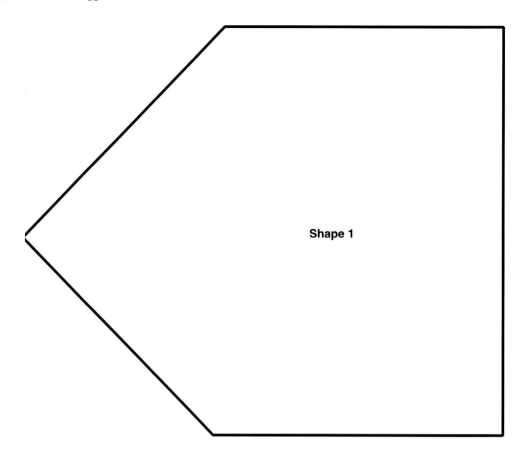

Shape 1

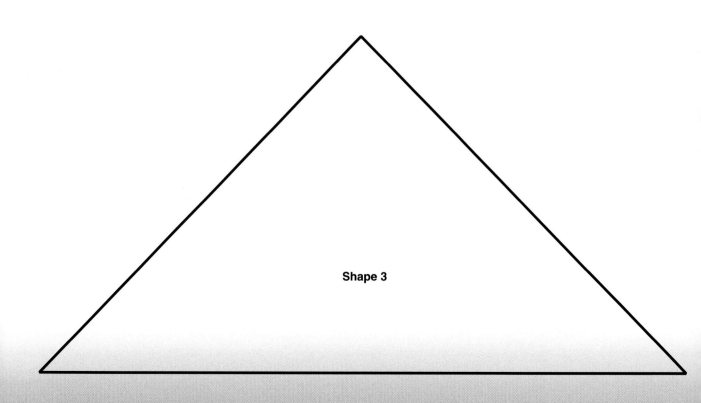

Shape 3

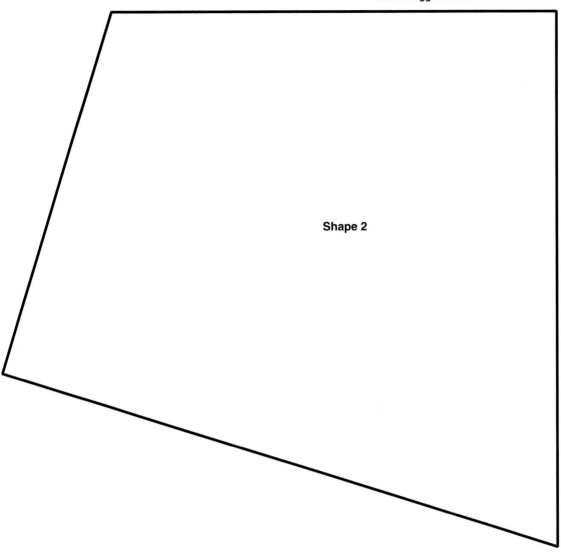

Shape 2

Pattern begins on page 1

Chapter 5
Quilts and More

Create a coordinated look for any bedroom in your home with these fun-to-stitch scrappy quilts and matching projects. In addition to colorful scrappy quilts for beds of all sizes, in this chapter you'll find runners, pillows, toys, valances, dresser scarves and more.

In This Chapter

Stripe Mosaic

By Judith Sandstrom

Bright fabric strips make up the fabric used in the triangles on this quick-and-easy quilt and table runner set which can be stitched up in a weekend.

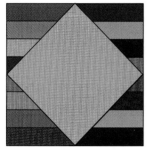

Stripe Mosaic
7 1/4" x 7 1/4" Block

Stripe Mosaic Quilt
Placement Diagram
87" x 101 1/2"

Project Specifications

Skill Level: Beginner

Quilt Size: 87" x 101 1/2"

Table Runner Size: 14 1/2" x 43 1/2"

Block Size: 7 1/4" x 7 1/4"

Number of Blocks: 71 whole blocks and 26 half blocks for quilt; 2 whole blocks and 8 half blocks for table runner

Materials

- 1/4 yard each 16 bright prints
- 6 1/2 yards muslin
- 6 yards 60"-wide backing fabric
- Batting 91" x 106" for quilt
- Batting 19" x 48" for table runner
- 15 yards self-made or purchased binding
- Neutral color all-purpose thread
- Basic sewing supplies and tools and rotary-cutting equipment

Making Blocks

Step 1. Cut the following from muslin: 75 squares 7 3/4" x 7 3/4"; 73 squares 5 5/8" x 5 5/8" for A; 26 rectangles 4 1/8" x 7 3/4" for B; 8 squares 4 1/8" x 4 1/8" for C; and 17 squares 6" x 6" for D.

Step 2. Cut each D square in half along one diagonal to make D triangles as shown in Figure 1.

Stripe Mosaic Table Runner
Placement Diagram
14 1/2" x 43 1/2"

Figure 1
Cut each D square in half along 1 diagonal to make D triangles.

Step 3. Cut five 1 1/2" by fabric width strips from each of the 16 bright prints.

Step 4. Arrange the eighty 1 1/2"-wide strips into 20 random groups of four strips each. Stitch the four strips from each group with right sides together along length to make 20 strip sets. Press seams open. *Note: Stitch each new strip in the opposite direction to minimize stretching of fabric.*

Step 5. Cut each strip set into nine 4 1/2" segments as shown in Figure 2 for a total of 180 squares.

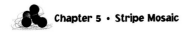
4 1/2"

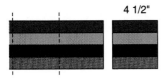

Figure 2
Cut each strip set into
nine 4 1/2" segments.

Step 6. Cut each square in half on one diagonal, cutting five squares from 10 strip sets in one direction to make E triangles and the remaining four squares in the opposite direction to make F triangles as shown in Figure 3. Cut the remaining 10 strip sets in half on one diagonal, cutting five squares to make F triangles and four squares to make E triangles from each strip set. You will need 180 each E and F triangles.

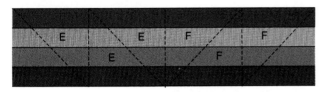

Figure 3
Cut squares from each strip in the direction
shown to make E and F triangles.

Step 7. Sew four different color E and F triangles to each A square, positioning E and F pieces as shown in Figure 4 to complete one block; press seams toward A. Repeat for 73 blocks.

Step 8. Sew an E and F triangle to two adjacent sides of a D triangle as shown in Figure 5 to complete one half block; press seams toward D. Repeat for 34 half blocks.

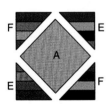

Figure 4
Sew 4 different color E
and F triangles to each A
square, positioning
triangle pieces as shown.

Figure 5
Sew an E and F
triangle to 2 adjacent
sides of a D triangle.

Making the Quilt

Step 1. Join six 7 3/4" x 7 3/4" muslin squares with five pieced blocks to make a row; sew a half block to each end as shown in Figure 6. Press seams open. Repeat for seven rows.

Step 2. Join five 7 3/4" x 7 3/4" muslin squares with six pieced blocks to make a row; sew a B rectangle to each end as shown in Figure 7. Press seams open; repeat for six rows.

Step 3. Join the rows beginning and ending with rows ending with half blocks; press seams open.

7 3/4" x 7 3/4"

Figure 6
Join six 7 3/4" x 7 3/4" muslin squares with 5 pieced blocks
to make a row; sew a half block to each end.

7 3/4" x 7 3/4"

Figure 7
Join five 7 3/4" x 7 3/4" muslin squares with 6 pieced
blocks to make a row; sew a B rectangle to each end.

Step 4. Join six half blocks with B and add C to each end to make top row as shown in Figure 8; repeat for bottom row. Press seams open

Figure 8
Join 6 half blocks with B and add C to each end to make top row.

Step 5. Sew one B-C-half-block row to the top and bottom of the pieced center; press seams open.

Step 6. Prepare a 91" x 106" backing piece from 60"-wide backing fabric.

Step 7. Prepare for quilting and quilt and bind referring to the General Instructions. *Note: The quilt shown was machine-quilted using off-white thread on the diagonal in one direction through each block.*

Making the Table Runner

Step 1. Join three 7 3/4" x 7 3/4" muslin squares with two whole blocks and two half blocks as shown in Figure 9; press seams open.

7 3/4" x 7 3/4"

Figure 9
Join three 7 3/4" x 7 3/4" muslin squares with
2 whole blocks and 2 half blocks as shown.

Figure 10
Join 3 half blocks with 2 B
and 2 C pieces as shown.

Step 2. Join three half blocks with two B and two C pieces as shown in Figure 10; repeat. Press seams open.

Step 3. Sew a B-C-half-block unit to each long side of the pieced section; press seams open.

Step 4. Cut a 19" x 48" backing piece from the 60"-wide backing fabric.

Step 5. Prepare table runner for quilting as in Step 7 for Making the Quilt. ◨

Scrappy Baby Quilt and Happy the Clown

By Judith Sandstrom

Any little girl will love this quilt with matching clown doll. The pastel colors will match most any decor.

Striped
6" x 6" Block

Project Specifications

Skill Level: Beginner

Quilt Size: 42 1/2" x 68"

Doll Size: Approximately 15" x 15"

Block Size: 6" x 6"

Number of Blocks: 40 for quilt; 8 for doll

Materials

- 1/4 yard each 12 pastel prints
- 1/3 yard beige-on-beige print
- 1 1/2 yards white-on-white print
- Backing 46" x 72"
- Batting 46" x 72"
- 5" x 5" square batting
- 6 1/2 yards self-made or purchased binding
- All-purpose thread to match fabrics
- Polyester fiberfill
- 1 1/2 yards 1/2"-wide flat white lace
- 1 1/4 yards 1/8"-wide elastic
- Brown 4-ply acrylic yarn
- Blue, brown and red permanent fabric pens
- Basic sewing supplies and tools and rotary-cutting equipment, wash-out pen or pencil

Scrappy Baby Quilt
Placement Diagram
42 1/2" x 68"

Happy the Clown
Placement Diagram
Approximately 15" x 15"

Scrappy Baby Quilt

Step 1. Cut the following from white-on-white print: 26 squares 6 1/2" x 6 1/2" for A; six squares 9 3/4" x 9 3/4"—cut each square on both diagonals to make B triangles; and two squares 5 1/8" x 5 1/8"—cut on one diagonal to make C triangles.

Step 2. Cut two strips each pastel print 2 1/2" by fabric width.

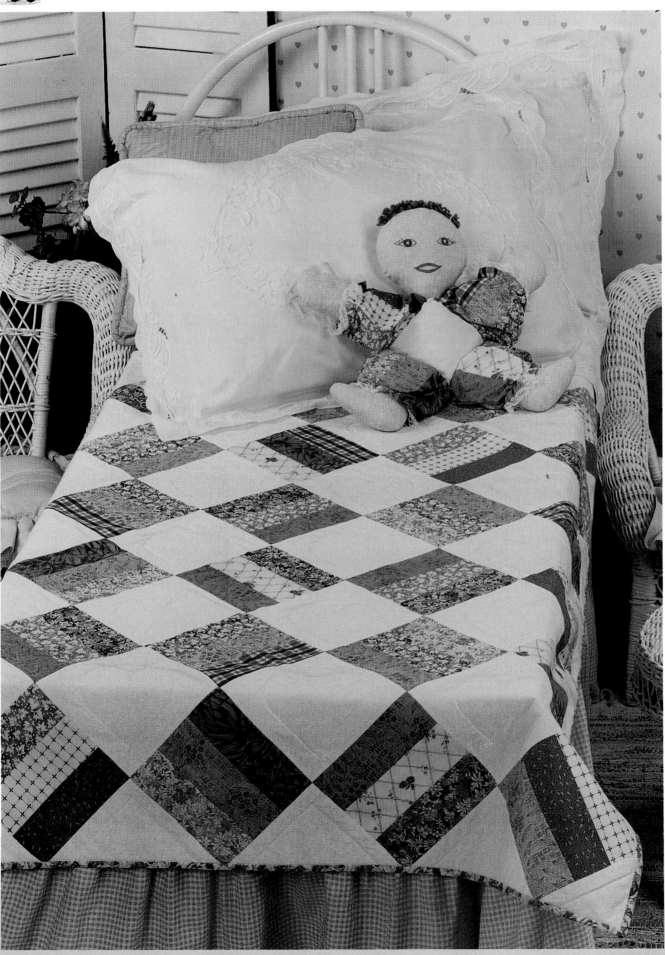

Step 3. Stitch pastel print strips with right sides together along length in eight different combinations of three strips each; press seams open.

Step 4. Subcut each strip set into 6 1/2" segments to make blocks; you will need 48 blocks. Set aside eight blocks for Happy the Clown.

Step 5. Arrange the remaining 40 blocks in diagonal rows with the A squares and B and C triangles as shown in Figure 1. Join blocks and triangles in diagonal rows; press seams open. Join rows to complete pieced top; press seams open.

Figure 1
Arrange the remaining 40 blocks in
diagonal rows with the A squares and
B and C triangles as shown.

Strip 6. Prepare quilt for quilting, finishing and binding referring to the General Instructions. *Note: The quilt was machine-quilted using the Heart Quilting Design given for quilt in the center of A squares.*

Happy the Clown

Step 1. Cut two 5" x 5" squares white-on-white print.

Step 2. Prepare templates for body pieces using pattern pieces given; cut as directed on each piece.

Step 3. Trace the facial features on the head/body piece using wash-out pen or pencil. Color in eyes with blue, mouth with red and eye outline with brown permanent fabric pen.

Step 4. Place two arm pieces right sides together; sew around leaving straight ends open. Clip curves and turn right side out; stuff lightly with polyester fiberfill. Baste

open end closed; repeat with remaining arm and leg pieces.

Step 5. With raw edges even, pin and baste one arm and one leg to the same side of the head/body front. With right sides together, pin and stitch head/body back to the front across arm and leg areas as shown in Figure 2. Turn right side out.

Figure 2
Sew arms and legs
to head/body piece.

Step 6. Repeat with second arm and leg on the other side of the head/body front. With right sides together, pin and stitch the head/body back to the front across the leg area and all the way around the head and neck, leaving the arm area open. Turn right side out; stuff the head and body with polyester fiberfill. Pin and hand-stitch the remaining arm opening closed.

Step 7. Using pieces of yarn about 10" long, wrap each piece around a pen or pencil eight times. Insert a threaded needle through each ply of yarn several times to hold it in place and attach it to the clown's head. The sample uses only 10 pieces of yarn along the seam line at the top of the head. Additional yarn may be added to cover the back of the head, if desired.

Step 8. Select a pleasing arrangement for four sets of two pastel print blocks set aside in Step 4 in Scrappy Baby Quilt referring to Figure 3 for positioning of blocks; mark bottom edges of each block to determine arm and leg openings. Turn under each bottom edge 1/4"; turn under again 1/4" and press.

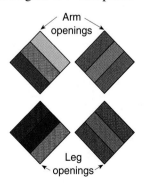

Figure 3
Arrange pieced blocks as shown to
determine leg and arm openings.

Step 9. Cut eight 6" pieces 1/2"-wide flat white lace, six 4" pieces and four 3 1/2" pieces 1/8"-wide elastic. Sew a piece of lace to the bottom edge of each block as shown in Figure 4. Sew a 4" piece of elastic 3/4" from fabric edge of each leg opening, and a 3 1/2" piece of elastic 3/4" from each arm opening, stretching elastic when stitching to fit from side to side as shown in Figure 5.

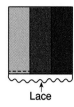

Figure 4
Sew a piece of lace to the bottom
edge of each block as shown.

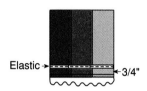

Figure 5
Sew a piece of elastic
3/4" from the edge of
leg opening as shown.

Step 10. Baste the 5" x 5" square batting to one of the white-on-white squares. Hand- or machine-quilt a heart in the center using design given.

Step 11. Mark a dot 3 1/4" from the lace end of each arm block for neck opening as shown in Figure 6. Machine-baste top edge of each block and gather slightly to fit edges of the 5" x 5" squares white-on-white print. With right sides together, pin and stitch two arm and two leg blocks to the quilted 5" x 5" white-on-white print square, leaving 1/4" open at each end of the squares to complete front; repeat for back using unquilted 5" x 5" square white-on-white print.

Step 12. Carefully fold neck edge under twice between marked dots and stitch a 4" piece of elastic from dot to dot on front; repeat on back.

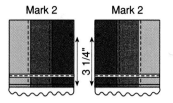

Figure 6
Mark a dot 3 1/4" from the end of
each arm block for neck opening.

Step 13. Join the two pieced units with right sides together leaving lace ends and neck edge of each block unstitched for arm, leg and neck openings as shown in Figure 7.

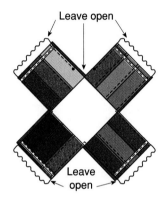

Figure 7
Join the 2 pieced units with right sides
together leaving lace ends and neck
edge of each block unstitched for arm,
leg and neck openings as shown.

Step 14. Place the completed cover on the stitched body legs first. ▄

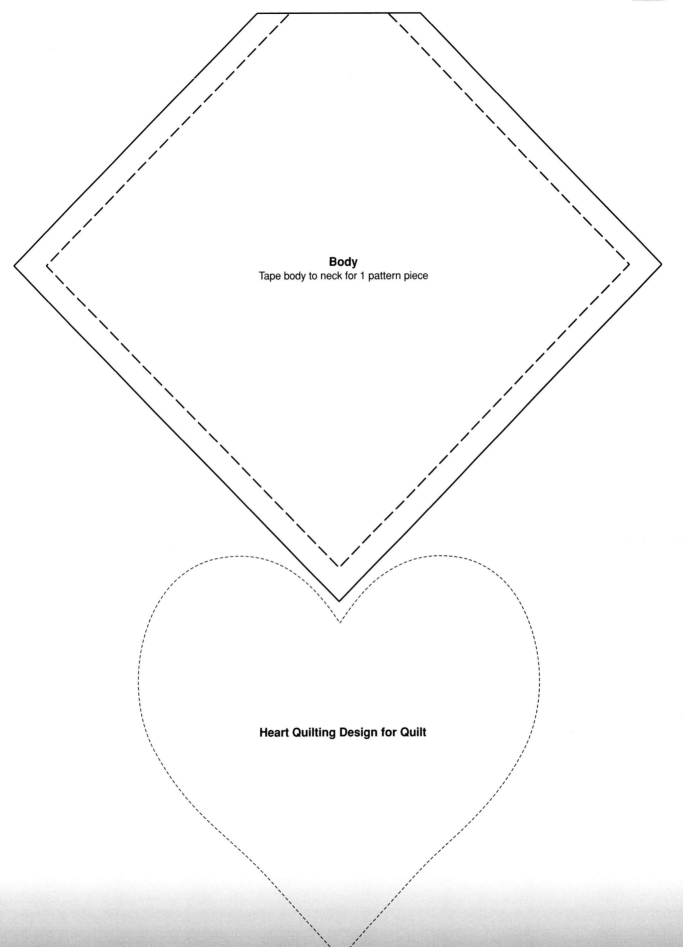

Body
Tape body to neck for 1 pattern piece

Heart Quilting Design for Quilt

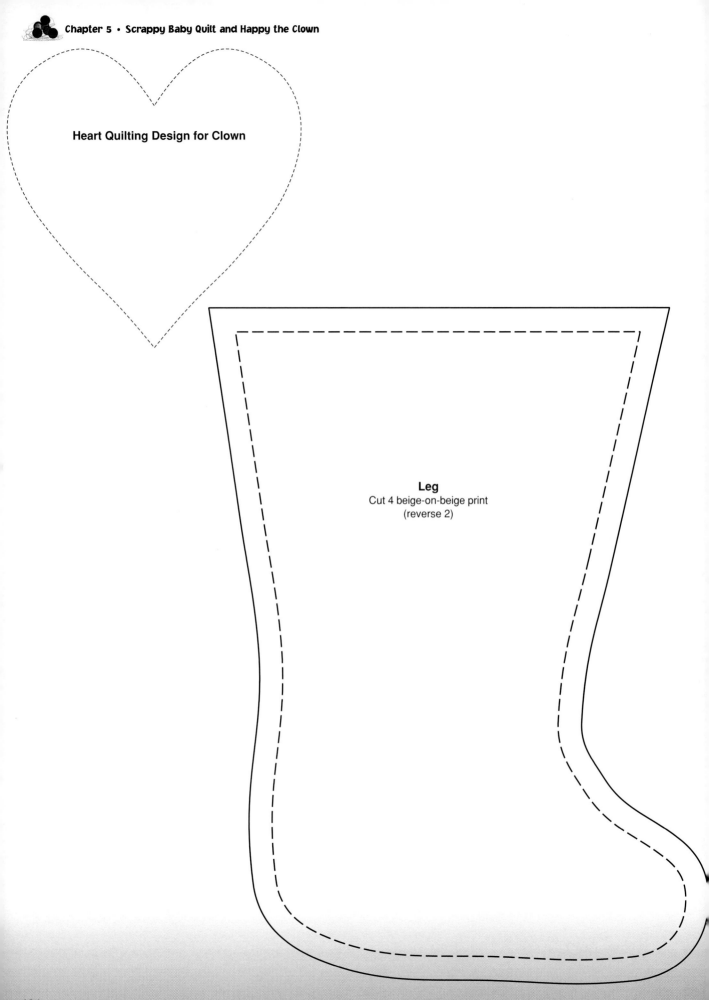

Heart Quilting Design for Clown

Leg
Cut 4 beige-on-beige print
(reverse 2)

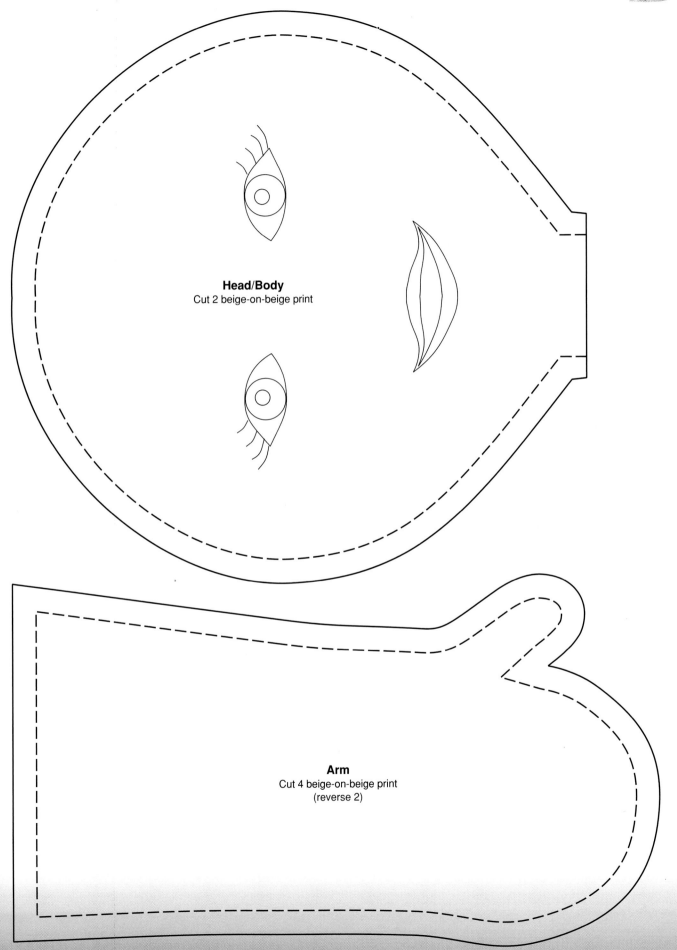

Head/Body
Cut 2 beige-on-beige print

Arm
Cut 4 beige-on-beige print
(reverse 2)

Bowl of Roses Quilt and Pillow

By Ruth M. Swasey

Look for antique scraps from the 1930s or reproduction prints to stitch up this beautiful appliqué quilt with matching pillow.

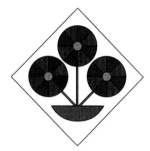

Bowl of Roses
14" x 14" Block

Project Specifications

Skill Level: Intermediate

Quilt Size: 72 1/4" x 92"

Pillow Size: 20" x 20"

Block Size: 14" x 14"

Number of Blocks: 18 for quilt; 1 for pillow

Materials

- 1/4 yard yellow print
- 1/2 yard total blue prints
- 3 1/2 yards total assorted pastel and red print scraps
- 5 yards white-on-white print
- Backing 76" x 96" for quilt
- 2 pieces backing 13 1/2" x 20 1/2" for pillow
- Batting 76" x 96"
- 20" pillow form
- 9 1/4 yards self-made or purchased binding
- All-purpose thread to match fabrics
- 6 1/2 yards 1/4"-wide light green bias tape for stems
- Basic sewing supplies and tools and rotary-cutting equipment

Bowl of Roses Quilt
Placement Diagram
72 1/4" x 92"

Bowl of Roses Quilt

Step 1. Cut 19 squares white-on-white print 14 1/2" x 14 1/2", three squares 21" x 21" and two squares 10 7/8" x 10 7/8". Cut the 21" x 21" square in half on both diagonals as shown in Figure 1 to make D triangles; set aside two D triangles for another project. Cut the 10 7/8" x 10 7/8" squares in half on one diagonal to make E triangles, again referring to Figure 1.

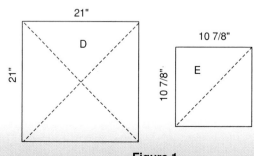

Figure 1
Cut squares as shown to make D and E triangles.

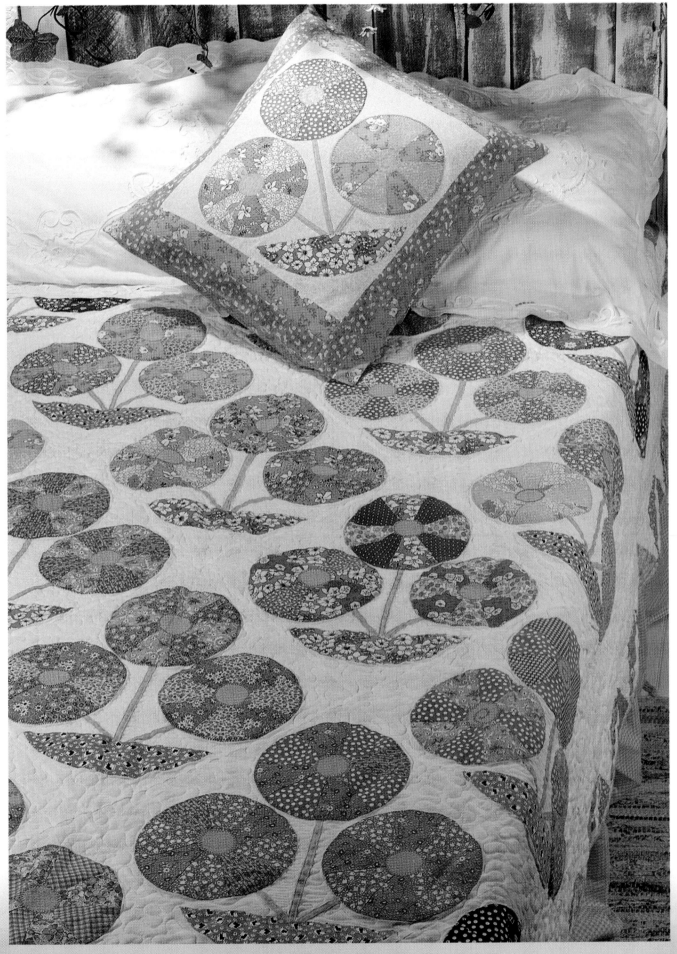

Step 2. Prepare templates using pattern pieces given; cut as directed on each piece for one block; repeat for 19 blocks.

Step 3. Join four each of two different fabric A pieces to make a circle as shown in Figure 2; press seams in one direction.

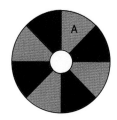

Figure 2
Join 4 each of 2 different fabric A
pieces to make a circle as shown.

Step 4. Turn under seam allowance all around; press. Turn under seam allowance on a B circle; center on the A unit. Appliqué in place by hand or machine; repeat for three A-B units.

Step 5. Cut one 6 1/2" and two 2 3/4" stem pieces from light green bias tape.

Step 6. Fold and crease one 14 1/2" x 14 1/2" square white-on-white print to find center. Pin C on one diagonal corner; tuck the three stem pieces under C as shown in Figure 3. Pin an A-B unit over the end of each stem piece. Hand- or machine-appliqué all pieces in place to complete one block; repeat for 18 blocks for quilt and one block for pillow.

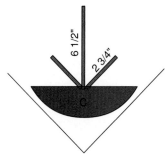

Figure 3
Tuck the 3 stem pieces
under C as shown.

Step 7. Lay out blocks with D and E triangles to make diagonal rows referring to Figure 4. Join blocks in rows; press seams in one direction. Join rows and add E triangles to the remaining corners to complete the pieced top; press seams in one direction.

Step 8. Cut two strips each 3" x 64 3/4" and 3" x 79 1/2". *Note: Border strips are cut along length of fabric in section remaining after cutting pieces in Step 1.* Sew the longer strips to opposite long sides and shorter strips to the top and bottom of the pieced center; press seams toward strips.

Figure 4
Lay out blocks with D and E
triangles to make diagonal rows.

Step 9. Cut five strips white-on-white print 4 7/8" by fabric width; subcut into 4 7/8" segments for F; you will need 39 segments. Cut each segment on one diagonal to make F triangles; you will need 78 F triangles.

Step 10. Cut forty 4 7/8" x 4 7/8" squares from assorted pastel scraps. Cut as in Step 9 to make F triangles.

Step 11. Sew a white-on-white print F triangle to a scrap triangle to make a square; repeat for 78 squares.

Step 12. Join 16 F units as shown in Figure 5; press seams in one direction. Repeat for two strips. Sew a strip to the top and bottom of the pieced center; press seams toward strips. Repeat with 23 F units for one side strip referring to the Placement Diagram; repeat for two strips. Sew to opposite long sides of pieced center; press seams toward strips.

Figure 5
Join 16 F units as shown to make a border strip.

Strip 13. Prepare quilt for quilting, finishing and binding referring to the General Instructions.

Bowl of Roses Pillow

Step 1. Cut two strips each two different colors 2" x 14 1/2" and 2" x 20 1/2".

Step 2. Sew two different same-length strips together along length; press seam in one direction. Repeat for two strip sets. Sew one strip set to opposite sides of the block pieced in Step 6 for the quilt. Repeat with remaining longer strips and sew to remaining sides; press seams toward strips.

Step 3. Fold under one 20 1/2" edge of each pillow backing piece 1/4"; press. Fold under 1/2" again; press and stitch to hem.

Step 4. Overlap finished edges of backing pieces 5" as shown in Figure 6; machine-baste along overlapped edges.

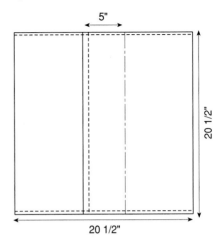

Figure 6
Overlap finished edges of backing pieces 5"; machine-baste to hold.

Step 5. Place pillow backing right sides together with bordered block. Stitch all around; turn right side out. Stuff pillow form inside through back opening to finish pillow. *Note: If desired batting and quilting may be added to the pillow top.*

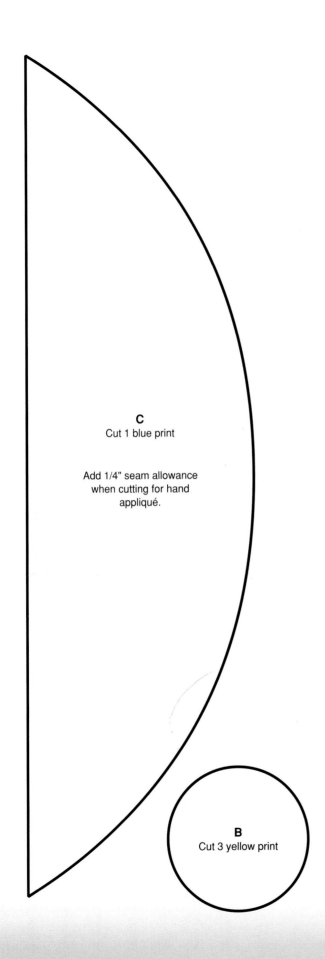

C
Cut 1 blue print

Add 1/4" seam allowance when cutting for hand appliqué.

B
Cut 3 yellow print

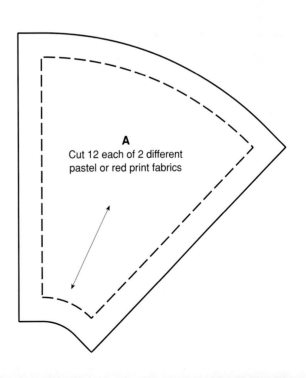

A
Cut 12 each of 2 different pastel or red print fabrics

Stars & Stripes Quilt and Dresser Scarf

By Ruth M. Swasey

Patriotic quilters will enjoy making this red-white-and-blue quilt and matching dresser scarf using the traditional LeMoyne Star block.

Stars & Stripes Quilt
Placement Diagram
84" x 97"

Dark LeMoyne Star
12" x 12" Block

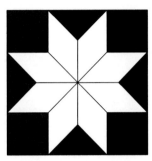

Light LeMoyne Star
12" x 12" Block

Project Specifications

Skill Level: Intermediate

Quilt Size: 84" x 97"

Dresser Scarf Size: 17" x 51"

Block Size: 12" x 12"

Number of Blocks: 12 light and 18 dark for quilt; 3 dark for dresser scarf

Materials

- 3 yards total assorted white-on-white prints
- 3 yards total assorted navy prints
- 4 yards red print
- 8 strips white-on-white print 2" by fabric width
- Backing 88" x 101" for quilt and 21" x 55" for dresser scarf
- Batting 88" x 101" for quilt and 21" x 55" for dresser scarf
- 10 1/2 yards self-made or purchased binding for quilt and 4 1/4 yards for dresser scarf
- All-purpose thread to match fabrics
- Basic sewing supplies and tools and rotary-cutting equipment

Quilt

Step 1. Prepare templates using pattern pieces given. Cut as directed on each piece for one block. Repeat cutting for 12 light and 18 dark blocks.

Step 2. To piece one block join two white-on-white or navy print A pieces along one seam, stopping at the seam line as shown in Figure 1; repeat for four units. Join two units; press seams as shown in Figure 2. Repeat for a second unit and join to complete the star design set in white-on-white or navy B and C pieces to complete one block. Repeat for 12 light and 18 dark blocks.

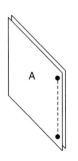

Figure 1
Join 2 white-on-white or navy print A pieces along 1 seam, stopping at the seam line as shown.

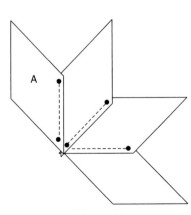

Figure 2
Join 2 units; press seams as shown.

Step 3. Cut 25 strips red print 3 1/2" x 12 1/2" for sashing strips.

Step 4. Join six dark blocks with five 3 1/2" x 12 1/2" red print sashing strips to make a row as shown in Figure 3; press seams toward sashing strips. Repeat for three dark rows and two light rows.

Figure 3
Join 6 dark blocks with five 3 1/2" x 12 1/2" red print sashing strips to make a row.

Step 5. Cut four strips red print 3 1/2" x 87 1/2" along length of fabric. Join the rows with these strips, alternating light and dark rows referring to the Placement Diagram; press seams toward strips.

Step 6. Cut two strips red print 6 1/2" x 87 1/2" along length of fabric. Sew a strip to opposite long sides of the pieced center; press seams toward strips.

Step 7. Cut one strip each red print 4 1/2" x 84 1/2" and 6 1/2" x 84 1/2" along length of fabric. Sew the 4 1/2"-wide strip to the top and the 6 1/2"-wide strip to the bottom of the pieced center; press seams toward strips.

Step 8. Prepare quilt for quilting, finishing and binding referring to the General Instructions.

Dresser Scarf

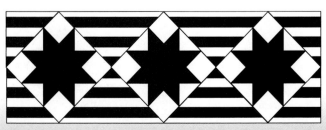

Stars & Stripes Dresser Scarf
Placement Diagram
17" x 51"

Step 1. Piece three dark LeMoyne Star blocks referring to Step 2 in Quilt Instructions.

Step 2. Cut six strips red print 2" by fabric width. Sew together with the eight 2"-wide strips white-on-white print to make two strip sets as shown in Figure 4; press seams in one direction.

Figure 4
Join strips as shown to make 2 strip sets.

Step 3. Prepare template for pieces D and E using pattern given; cut referring to Figure 5.

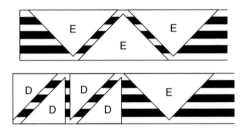

Figure 5
Cut D and E pieces from strip sets as shown.

Step 4. Arrange D and E pieces with pieced blocks in diagonal rows referring to Figure 6; join in rows. Press seams toward D and E. Join the diagonal rows to complete pieced top.

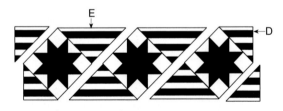

Figure 6
Arrange D and E pieces with pieced blocks in diagonal rows.

Step 5. Prepare dresser scarf for quilting, finishing and binding referring to the General Instructions. ◼

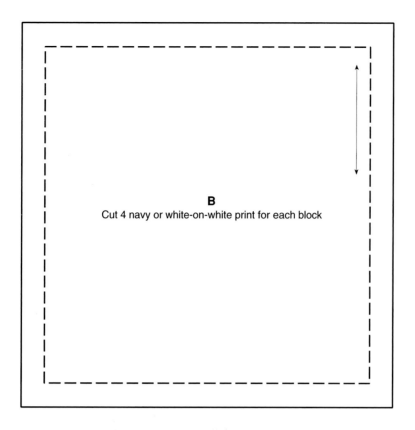

B
Cut 4 navy or white-on-white print for each block

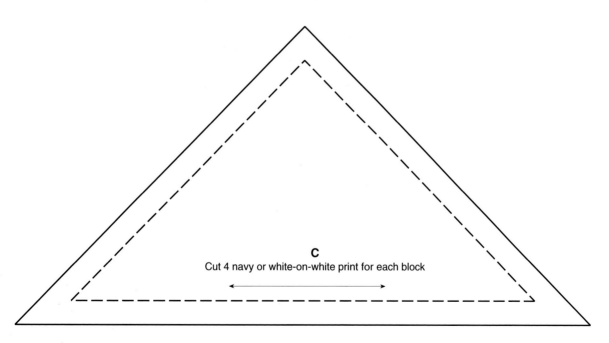

C
Cut 4 navy or white-on-white print for each block

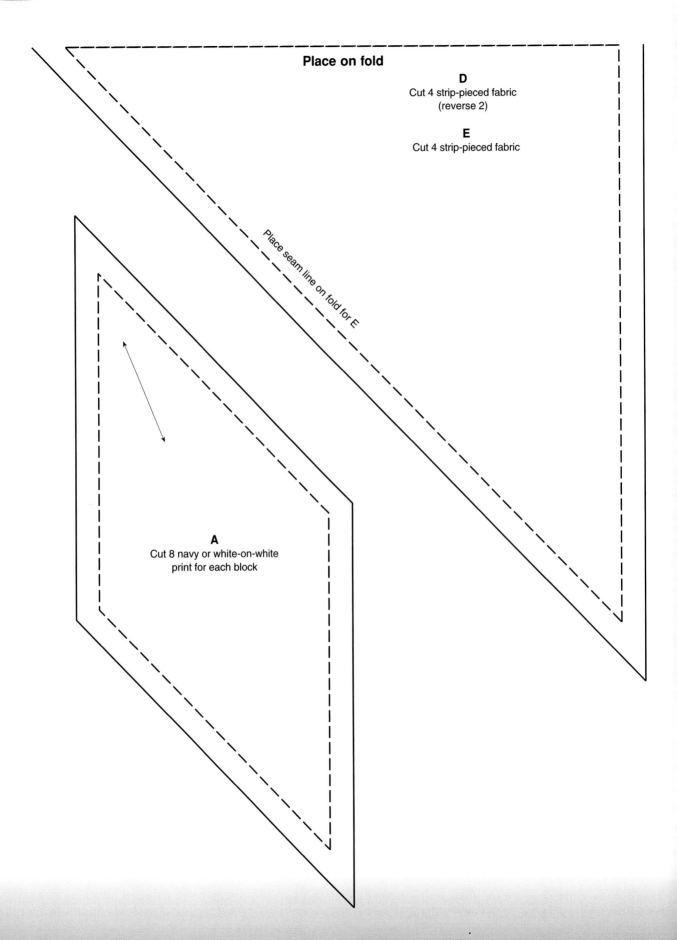

Place on fold

D
Cut 4 strip-pieced fabric
(reverse 2)

E
Cut 4 strip-pieced fabric

Place seam line on fold for E

A
Cut 8 navy or white-on-white
print for each block

Crosswinds Quilt and Valance

By Ruth M. Swasey

Large floral prints combine with green and flowery-colored solids to give this quilt the feel of a walk through the garden.

Crosswinds
5" x 5" Block
10" x 10" Block

Project Specifications

Skill Level: Intermediate

Quilt Size: 100" x 100"

Valance Size: 13" x 60"

Block Size: 10" x 10" and 5" x 5"

Number of Blocks: 81 large and 4 small for quilt; 6 large for valance

Materials

- 2 1/2 yards total solid scraps
- 4 1/4 yards white-on-white print
- 5 1/2 yards total large floral print scraps
- Backing 104" x 104" for quilt and 13 1/2" x 60 1/2" for valance
- Batting 104" x 104"
- 11 1/2 yards self-made or purchased binding
- All-purpose thread to match fabrics
- Basic sewing supplies and tools and rotary-cutting equipment

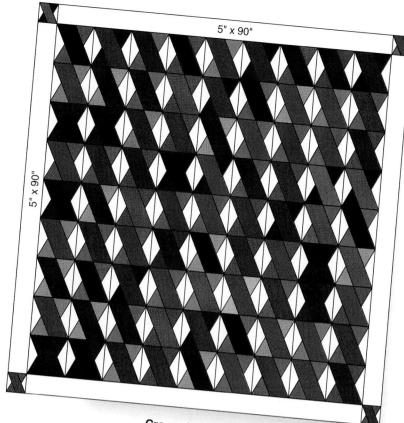

Crosswinds Quilt
Placement Diagram
100" x 100"

Crosswinds Quilt

Step 1. Prepare templates using pattern pieces given; cut as directed on each piece. Repeat for 81 large blocks for quilt, six large blocks for valance and four small blocks for quilt.

Step 2. To piece one large block, sew A to C; repeat. Sew an A-C unit to each long side of B as shown in Figure 1 to complete one block; press. Repeat for 87 large blocks. Set aside six blocks for valance.

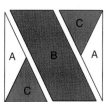

Figure 1
Sew A-C units to long sides of B to
complete 1 large block; repeat with D-E
units and F to complete 1 small block.

Step 3. Join blocks in nine rows of nine blocks each; press seams in one direction. Join rows to complete pieced center; press seams in one direction.

Step 4. To piece one small block, sew D to E; repeat. Sew a D-E unit to each long side of F to complete one block again referring to Figure 1; press. Repeat for four small blocks.

Step 5. Cut and piece four strips each 5 1/2" x 90 1/2". Sew a strip to two opposite sides; press seams toward strips. Sew a small block to each end of the remaining two strips referring to the Placement Diagram for positioning of blocks. Sew strips to the remaining sides; press seams toward strips.

Strip 6. Prepare quilt for quilting, finishing and binding referring to the General Instructions.

Crosswinds Valance

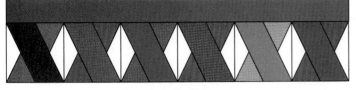

Crosswinds Valance
Placement Diagram
13" x 60"

Step 1. Join the six large blocks pieced in Step 2 for quilt referring to the Placement Diagram for positioning of blocks.

Step 2. Cut and piece a 3 1/2" x 60 1/2" strip floral print. Sew this strip to one long edge of the pieced block strip with right sides together; press seam toward strip.

Step 3. Place the 13 1/2" x 60 1/2" valance backing piece right sides together with the pieced strip. Sew all around leaving 5" open on one end and a 1 1/2" opening 1" down from each top edge as shown in Figure 2. Turn right side out; press. Hand-stitch 5" opening closed. Turn under seam allowance in 1 1/2" openings; hand-stitch in place.

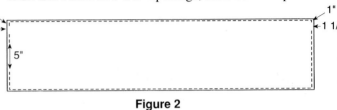

Figure 2
Stitch all around leaving openings as shown.

Step 4. Stitch 1" down across top edge and 1 1/2" from this line of stitching for rod opening to finish. *Note: These stitching lines should correspond with openings left in Step 4.* ◼

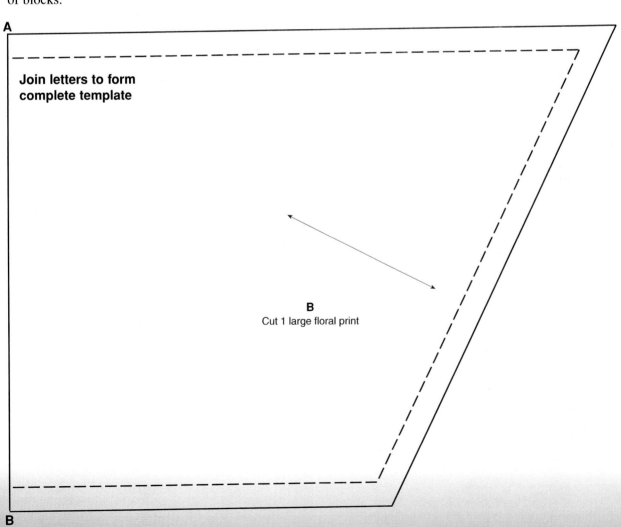

A

Join letters to form
complete template

B
Cut 1 large floral print

B

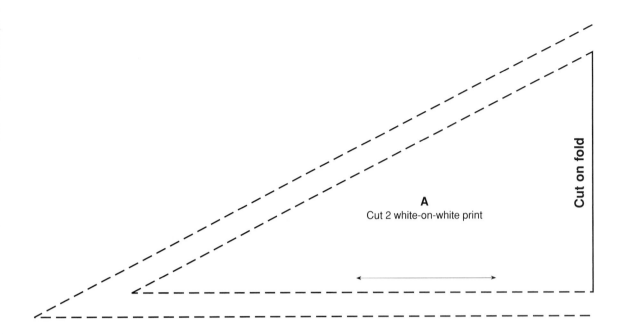

A
Cut 2 white-on-white print

Cut on fold

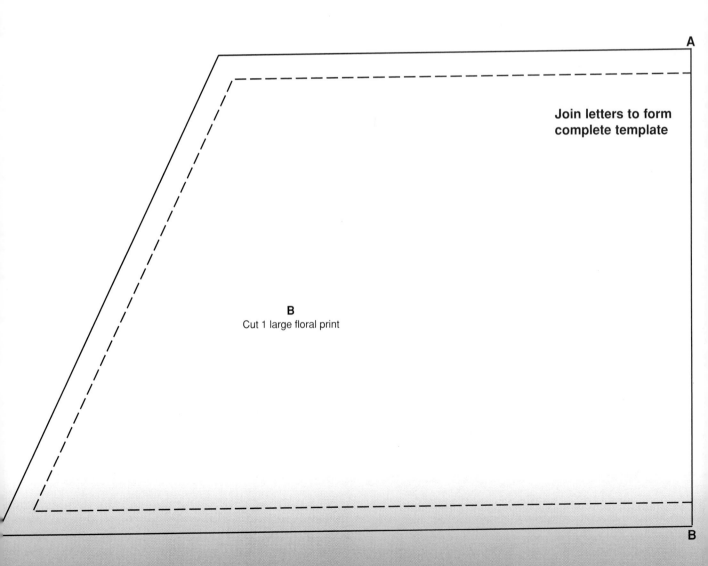

A

Join letters to form
complete template

B
Cut 1 large floral print

B

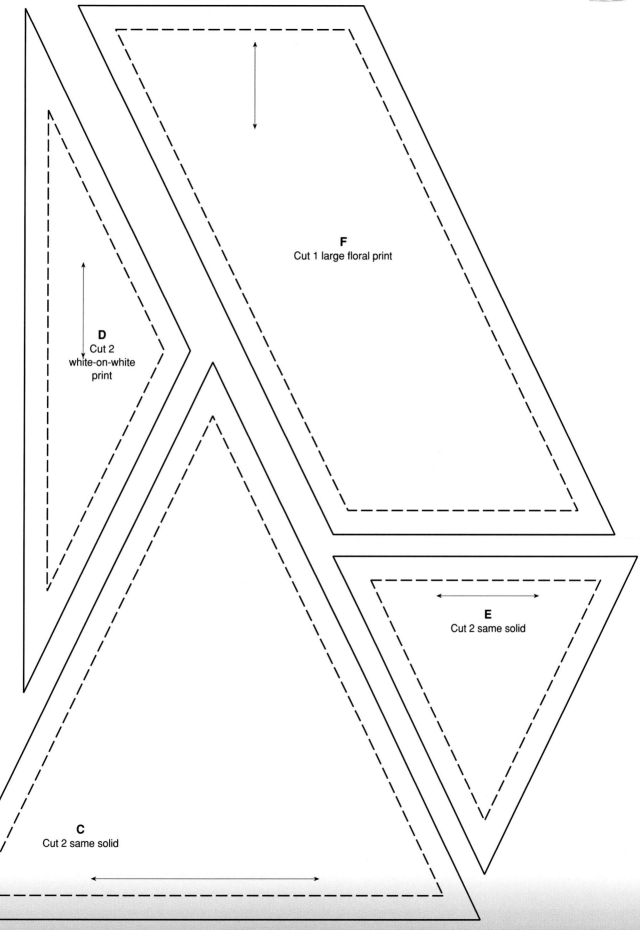

F
Cut 1 large floral print

D
Cut 2
white-on-white
print

E
Cut 2 same solid

C
Cut 2 same solid

Secret Star Ensemble

By Judith Sandstrom

Coordinate a bedroom with a valance and table topper to match the quilt using this easy pattern and a variety of colored prints.

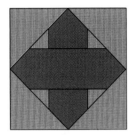

Secret Star
12" x 12" Block

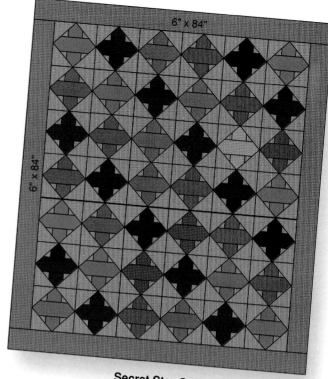

Secret Star Quilt
Placement Diagram
84" x 96"

Project Specifications

Skill Level: Beginner

Quilt Size: 84" x 96"

Valance: 14 1/2" x 48"

Table Topper: 24" x 24"

Table Cover: 62" diameter

Curtains: 23" x 51 1/2"

Block Size: 12" x 12"

Number of Blocks: 42 for quilt, 4 for valance and 4 for table topper

Materials

- 1/6 yard each of 5 green, 6 blue and 6 rose prints for quilt blocks
- 1/3 yard each of 2 green, 1 blue and 1 rose print (used in blocks for quilt, valance and table topper)
- 1 yard blue print for ruffle and drapery tie-backs
- 4 3/4 yards 54"-wide yellow floral print decorator fabric (quilt borders, table topper and drapery panels for one window—add 1 1/2 yards for each additional window)
- 8 yards pale yellow print for background
- Backing 88" x 100" for quilt and 28" x 28" for table topper

- Batting 88" x 100" for quilt; 28" x 28" for table topper
- 10 1/2 yards self-made or purchased binding for quilt and 3 1/4 yards for table topper
- All-purpose thread to match fabrics
- Double curtain rod and decorative tie-back hardware
- Basic sewing supplies and tools and rotary-cutting equipment

Secret Star Quilt

Step 1. Prewash all fabrics.

Step 2. Cut 25 strips pale yellow print 4 1/2" by fabric width. Cut eight 4 1/2" segments from each strip for A.

Step 3. Cut 17 strips pale yellow print 6 7/8" by fabric width; cut each strip into 6 7/8" segments. Cut 100 of these square segments in half on one diagonal to make 200 B triangles.

Step 4. Cut a 4 1/2" by fabric width strip from each of the 1/8-yard prints. Cut two 4 1/2" x 12 1/2" rectangles and four 4 1/2" segments from strips.

Step 5. Cut two 4 1/2" by fabric width strips from each of the 1/4-yard prints. Cut four 4 1/2" x 12 1/2" rectangles and eight 4 1/2" segments from each strip.

Step 6. To make one block, sew a colored square

between two A squares, press seams open. Repeat to make two units as shown in Figure 1.

Figure 1
Sew a colored square
between 2 A squares.

Step 7. Stitch a matching 4 1/2" x 12 1/2" colored piece between the two pieced units as shown in Figure 2; press seams open. Repeat for 50 squares.

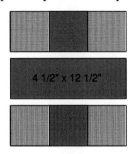

Figure 2
Stitch a matching 4 1/2" x
12 1/2" colored piece
between the 2 pieced units.

Step 8. Pin a B triangle to opposite corners of one unit exactly 6 1/4" from the edge of the pieced unit as shown in Figure 3. Stitch along the diagonal of the triangle with a 1/4" seam allowance as shown in Figure 4.

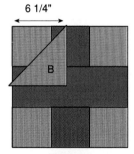

Figure 3
Pin a B triangle to opposite
corners of 1 unit exactly 6 1/4"
from the edge of the pieced
unit as shown.

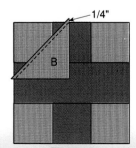

Figure 4
Stitch along the diagonal
of the triangle with a 1/4"
seam allowance.

Step 9. Press B triangles to the right side and check that they line up evenly with underneath unit layer. Trim off excess from under B leaving a 1/4" seam allowance as shown in Figure 5. Repeat on each corner of the square to complete one Secret Star block as shown in Figure 6. Repeat for 50 blocks. Set aside eight blocks for valance and table topper. *Note: Save the cut-off sections to make a coordinating wall quilt or pillows, if desired.*

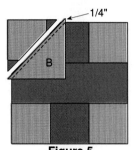

Figure 5
Trim off excess from under
B leaving a 1/4" seam
allowance as shown.

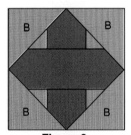

Figure 6
Repeat on each
corner of the square
to complete 1 Secret
Star block.

Step 10. Arrange blocks in seven rows of six blocks each, placing colors in a diagonal arrangement using 14 blocks in each color. Join blocks in rows; press seams open. Join rows to complete pieced center; press seams open.

Step 11. Cut four strips 6 1/2" x 84 1/2" strips along the length of the yellow floral print. Sew to opposite long sides and then to to the top and bottom; press seams toward strips.

Step 12. Prepare quilt for quilting, finishing and binding referring to the General Instructions. *Note: The quilt shown was machine-quilted 1/4" beyond seams joining colored print pieces with pale yellow print pieces.*

Secret Star Table Topper & Table Cover

Step 1. Join two green, one rose and one blue print blocks in two rows of two blocks each referring to the Placement Diagram; press seams open. Join the two rows to complete the pieced center; press seams open.

Step 2. Prepare for quilting and finishing as in Step 12 for Secret Star Quilt.

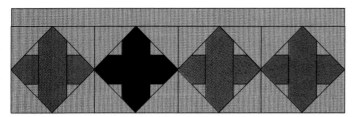

Secret Star Valance
Placement Diagram

Step 3. Cut a 1 1/2-yard piece from uncut end of yellow floral print. Fold the cut piece in half across length and width to make a square, keeping all edges even. Measure and mark 26" from the center point at 1 1/2" intervals as shown in Figure 7. Connect the dots to make a solid line; cut along the line to make a circle.

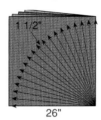

Figure 7
Measure and mark
26" from the center
point at 1 1/2"
intervals as shown.

Step 4. Cut five strips 6" by fabric width blue print. Join the strips with right sides together along short ends to make one long strip; sew remaining seam to make a tube. Press seams open.

Step 5. Using a wide machine stitch, sew two lines of gathering stitches along one long edge of strip. Pull threads to gather. Adjust gathers evenly and pin to the yellow floral print circle with right sides together for ruffle. Stitch in place; fold down and press.

Step 6. Fold under the raw edge 1/4"; press. Turn under another 1/4" and stitch for hem to finish.

Secret Star Valance & Drapery Panel

Secret Star Table Topper
Placement Diagram
24" x 24"

Step 1. Join two green, one rose and one blue print blocks in one row referring to the Placement Diagram; press seams open.

Step 2. Cut and piece one rectangle pale yellow print 12 1/2" x 48 1/2" for valance lining.

Step 3. Place lining right sides together with block row; stitch around two short sides and one long side. Turn right side out; press.

Step 4. Cut a 5 1/2" x 50" strip pale yellow print for rod pocket piece. Fold under one long edge 1/4"; press. Fold each short end under 1"; press and hand-stitch in place.

Step 5. Pin and stitch the rod pocket piece right sides and raw edges together with the lined valance; stitch. Turn the rod pocket to the back; hand-stitch in place to cover seam to finish valance.

Step 6. Cut two pieces yellow floral print 26" x 54" along length of section left after cutting quilt borders. Turn each 54" side under 1/4"; press. Turn under again 1" for side hems. Hand- or machine-stitch in place. Fold both 26" ends under 1/4"; press. Turn under again 1 1/4" for hem; machine stitch in place to make rod pocket and bottom hem to finish.

Step 7. Cut two 3 1/2" x 21" pieces blue print for tie-backs. Fold each strip with right sides together along length. Stitch along all edges, leaving a 4" opening in the center; turn right side out; press. Hand-stitch opening closed to finish. ◼

Bright Triangles

By Lucy Fazely

Two different quilts can be made using the same pieced units to create two different blocks—each one using triangle squares to make the design.

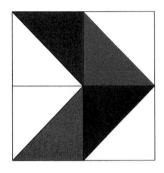

Bright Triangles
8" x 8" Block

Bright Triangles 1
Placement Diagram
72" x 80"

Project notes

The list of materials will make one quilt. To make matching quilts with the same fabrics but different designs as shown purchase double the fabric listed. One quilt is bordered with purple and the other with royal blue.

Project Specifications

Skill Level: Beginner

Quilt Size: 72" x 80"

Block Size: 8" x 8"

Number of Blocks: 72

Materials

- 1/3 yard each of 18 bright mottled or print fabrics
- 4 1/4 yards white-on-white print
- 1 1/4 yards purple or royal blue mottled
- 2 1/4 yards 108"-wide backing fabric
- Batting 76" x 84"
- 9 yards self-made or purchased binding
- Neutral color all-purpose thread
- Basic sewing supplies and tools, masking tape, rotary-cutting equipment and fine-point pencil

Bright Triangles 2
Placement Diagram
72" x 80"

Bright Triangles 1

Step 1. Cut 32 strips white-on-white print 4 1/2" by fabric width; subcut each strip into 4 1/2" segments; you will need 288 segments.

Step 2. Cut two strips from each bright print or mottled fabric 4 1/2" by fabric width; subcut each strip into 4 1/2" segments to make 16 segments of each color to total 288 segments.

Step 3. Draw a diagonal line on the wrong side of each white-on-white print square using a fine-point pencil.

Step 4. Lay a white-on-white square on a bright print square with right sides together; stitch on marked line. Trim seam allowance to 1/4" as shown in Figure 1. Press pieces open with seam toward bright print side. Repeat for 288 units.

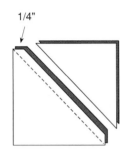

Figure 1
Trim seam allowance to 1/4"

Step 5. Join four segments as shown in Figure 2 to make a Bright Triangles block; repeat for 72 blocks.

Figure 2
Join 4 segments as
shown to make a Bright
Triangles block.

Step 6. Join eight blocks to make a row as shown in Figure 3; press seams in one direction. Repeat for nine rows.

Figure 3
Join 8 blocks to make a row.

Step 7. Join rows to complete pieced center; press seams in one direction.

Step 8. Cut and piece four strips 4 1/2" x 72 1/2" purple mottled. Sew two strips to opposite long sides and then to the top and bottom; press seams toward strips.

Step 9. Prepare quilt for quilting, finishing and binding referring to the General Instructions.

Bright Triangles 2

Step 1. Follow Steps 1–5 for Bright Triangles 1.

Step 2. Join eight blocks as shown in Figure 4; press seams in one direction. Repeat for nine rows.

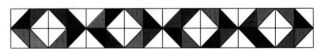

Figure 4
Join 8 blocks to make a row.

Step 3. Finish quilt referring to Steps 7–9 for Bright Triangles 1. ◼

Jumbles Lap Quilt and Pillow

By Holly Daniels

Challenge yourself to use up to 69 different scraps from your stash in this colorful quilt and pillow set. The pillow features a flap opening on back for easy laundering of pillow top.

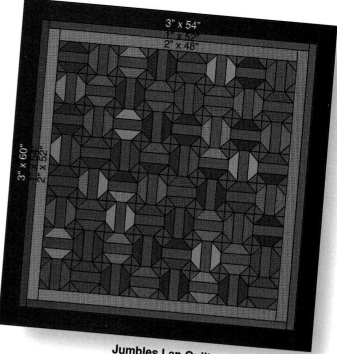

Jumbles Lap Quilt
Placement Diagram
60" x 60"

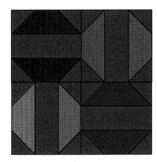

Jumbles
12" x 12" Block

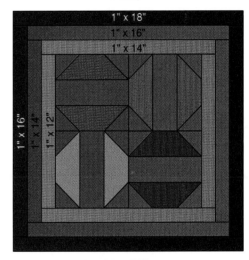

Jumbles Pillow
Placement Diagram
18" x 18"

Project Specifications

Skill Level: Beginner

Quilt Size: 60" x 60"

Pillow Size: 18" x 18"

Block Size: 12" x 12"

Number of Blocks: 16 for quilt; 1 for pillow

Materials

- 68 scraps 6" x 7" or 2 yards total assorted scraps
- 1/2 yard yellow print
- 3/4 yard red print
- 2 1/2 yards blue print
- Backing 64" x 64" for quilt; 2 pieces 12 1/2" x 18 1/2" for pillow
- Batting 64" x 64" for quilt; 20" x 20" for pillow
- 7 yards self-made or purchased binding
- All-purpose thread to match fabrics
- Clear nylon monofilament
- 18" x 18" pillow form
- Basic sewing supplies and tools and rotary-cutting equipment

Jumbles Lap Quilt

Step 1. Cut 12 strips blue print 2 1/2" by fabric width. Cut each strip into 6 1/2" segments for A; you will need 68 A segments.

Step 2. Cut each of the 6" x 7" scrap pieces into two 2 1/2" x 6 1/2" pieces for B.

Step 3. Sew a B piece to two opposite sides of A as shown in Figure 1; press seams toward B.

Figure 1
Sew a B piece to 2
opposite sides of A.

Step 4. Cut 17 strips blue print 2 1/2" by fabric width. Cut each strip into 2 1/2" segments for C squares; you will need 272 C squares.

Step 5. Lay a C square right sides together on one corner of an A-B unit; stitch along the diagonal of C referring to Figure 2; repeat on each corner referring to Figure 3.

Figure 2
Lay a C square right sides together on 1 corner of an A-B unit; stitch along the diagonal of C.

Figure 3
Repeat on each corner.

Step 6. Trim seam allowance to 1/4" on each corner; press C pieces to the right side to complete one block. Repeat for 68 units.

Step 7. Join four A-B-C units to complete one block as shown in Figure 4; repeat for 17 blocks. Set aside one block for pillow.

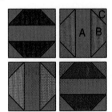

Figure 4
Join 4 A-B-C units to complete 1 block as shown.

Step 8. Arrange 16 blocks in four rows of four blocks each referring to the Placement Diagram for positioning of blocks. Join blocks in rows; join rows to complete pieced center. Press seams in one direction.

Step 9. Cut and piece two strips each yellow print 2 1/2" x 48 1/2" and 2 1/2" x 52 1/2". Sew the shorter strips to the top and bottom and longer strips to opposite sides; press seams toward strips.

Step 10. Cut and piece two strips each blue print 1 1/2" x 52 1/2" and 1 1/2" x 54 1/2". Sew the shorter strips to the top and bottom and longer strips to opposite sides; press seams toward strips.

Step 11. Cut and piece two strips each red print 3 1/2" x 54 1/2" and 3 1/2" x 60 1/2". Sew the shorter strips to the top and bottom and longer strips to opposite sides; press seams toward strips.

Step 12. Prepare quilt for quilting, finishing and binding referring to the General Instructions. *Note: The quilt*

was machine-quilted in the ditch of seams using clear nylon monofilament in the top of the machine and neutral color all-purpose thread in the bobbin.

Jumbles Pillow

Step 1. Cut two strips each yellow print 1 1/2" x 12 1/2" and 1 1/2" x 14 1/2". Sew the shorter strips to two opposite sides of the block set aside in Step 7 for Jumbles Lap Quilt; sew longer strips to remaining sides. Press seams toward strips.

Step 2. Cut two strips each blue print 1 1/2" x 14 1/2" and 1 1/2" x 16 1/2". Sew the shorter strips to two opposite sides and longer strips to remaining sides of the pillow block. Press seams toward strips.

Step 3. Cut two strips each red print 1 1/2" x 16 1/2" and 1 1/2" x 18 1/2". Sew the shorter strips to two opposite sides and longer strips to remaining sides of the pillow block. Press seams toward strips.

Step 4. Place 20" x 20" batting piece on the wrong side of the pillow top; pin or baste to hold. Quilt as desired by hand or machine. *Note: The sample shown was machine-quilted in a 2" grid pattern using clear nylon monofilament in the top of the machine and neutral color all-purpose thread in the bobbin.* Trim excess batting.

Step 5. Press one 18 1/2" edge of each 12 1/2" x 18 1/2" pillow backing piece under 1/4"; turn under again 1/2" and stitch in place. Lay backing pieces down on flat surface; overlap hemmed edges 5". Baste overlapped edges to hold as shown in Figure 5.

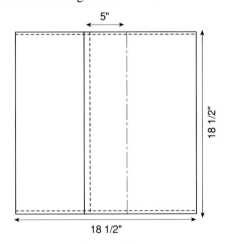

Figure 5
Overlap hemmed edges 5". Baste overlapped edges to hold as shown.

Step 6. Place pillow back right sides together with pillow front; stitch all around outside edges. Turn right side out through opening on backing pieces. Insert pillow form. ◼

Quiltmaking Basics

Materials & Supplies

Fabrics

Fabric Choices. Quilts and quilted projects combine fabrics of many types, depending on the project. It is best to combine same-fiber-content fabrics when making quilted items.

Buying Fabrics. One hundred percent cotton fabrics are recommended for making quilts. Choose colors similar to those used in the quilts shown or colors of your own preference. Most quilt designs depend more on contrast of values than on the colors used to create the design.

Preparing the Fabric for Use. Fabrics may be prewashed or not, depending on your preference. Whether you do or don't, be sure your fabrics are colorfast and won't run onto each other when washed after use.

Fabric Grain. Fabrics are woven with threads going in a crosswise and lengthwise direction. The threads cross at right angles—the more threads per inch, the stronger the fabric.

The crosswise threads will stretch a little. The lengthwise threads will not stretch at all. Cutting the fabric at a 45-degree angle to the crosswise and lengthwise threads produces a bias edge which stretches a great deal when pulled (Figure 1).

If templates are given with patterns in this book, pay careful attention to the grain lines marked with arrows. These arrows indicate that the piece should be placed on the lengthwise grain with the arrow running on one thread. Although it is not necessary to examine the fabric and find a thread to match to,

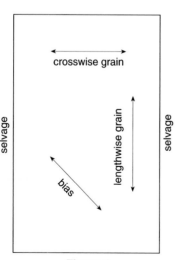

Figure 1
Drawing shows lengthwise, crosswise and bias threads.

it is important to try to place the arrow with the lengthwise grain of the fabric (Figure 2).

Thread

For most piecing, good-quality cotton or cotton-covered polyester is the thread of choice. Inexpensive polyester threads are not recommended because they can cut the fibers of cotton fabrics.

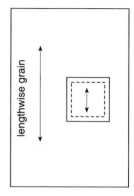

Figure 2
Place the template with marked arrow on the lengthwise grain of the fabric.

Choose a color thread that will match or blend with the fabrics in your quilt. For projects pieced with dark and light color fabrics choose a neutral thread color, such as a medium gray, as a compromise between colors. Test by pulling a sample seam.

Batting

Batting is the material used to give a quilt loft or thickness. It also adds warmth.

Batting size is listed in inches for each pattern to reflect the size needed to complete the quilt according to the instructions. Purchase the size large enough to cut the size you need for the quilt of your choice.

Some qualities to look for in batting are drapeability, resistance to fiber migration, loft and softness.

If you are unsure which kind of batting to use, purchase the smallest size batting available in the type you'd like to try. Test each sample on a small project. Choose the batting that you like working with most and that will result in the type of quilt you need.

Tools & Equipment

There are few truly essential tools and little equipment required for quiltmaking. The basics include needles (hand-sewing and quilting betweens), pins (long, thin sharp pins are best), sharp scissors or shears, a thimble, template materials (plastic or cardboard), marking tools (chalk marker, water-erasable pen and a No. 2 pencil are a few) and a quilting frame or hoop. For piecing and/or quilting by machine, add a sewing machine to the list.

Other sewing basics such as a seam ripper, pincushion, measuring tape and an iron are also necessary. For choosing colors or quilting designs for your quilt, or for designing your own quilt, it is helpful to have graph paper, tracing paper, colored pencils or markers and a ruler on hand.

For making strip-pieced quilts, a rotary cutter, mat and specialty rulers are often used. We recommend an ergonomic rotary cutter, a large self-healing mat and several rulers. If you can choose only one size, a 6" x 24" marked in 1/8" or 1/4" increments is recommended.

Construction Methods

Templates

Traditional Templates. While many quilt instructions in this book use rotary-cut strips and quick-sewing methods, a few patterns require templates. Templates are like the pattern pieces used to sew a garment. They are used to cut the fabric pieces which make up the quilt top. There are two types—templates that include a 1/4" seam allowance and those that don't.

Choose the template material and the pattern. Transfer the pattern shapes to the template material with a sharp No. 2 lead pencil. Write the pattern name, piece letter or number, grain line and number to cut for one block or whole quilt on each piece as shown in Figure 3.

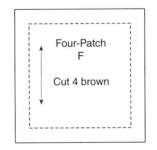

Four-Patch
F

Cut 4 brown

Figure 3
Mark each template with the pattern name and piece identification.

Some patterns require a reversed piece (Figure 4). These patterns are labeled with an R after the piece letter; for example, A and AR. To reverse a template, first cut it with the labeled side up and then with the labeled side down. Compare these to the right and left fronts of a blouse. When making a

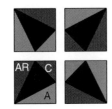

AR   C

A

Figure 4
This pattern uses reversed pieces.

garment, you accomplish reversed pieces when cutting the pattern on two layers of fabric placed with right sides together. This can be done when cutting templates as well.

If cutting one layer of fabric at a time, first trace the template onto the backside of the fabric with the marked side down; turn the template over with the marked side up to make reverse pieces.

Appliqué patterns given in this book do not include a seam allowance. Most designs are given in one drawing rather than individual pieces. This saves space while giving you the complete design to trace on the background block to help with placement of the pieces later. Make templates for each shape using the drawing for exact size. Remember to label each piece as for piecing templates.

For hand appliqué, add a seam allowance when cutting pieces from fabric. You may trace the template with label side up on the right side of the fabric if you are careful to mark lightly. The traced line is then the guide for turning the edges under when stitching.

If you prefer to mark on the wrong side of the fabric, turn the template over if you want the pattern to face the same way it does on the page.

For machine appliqué, a seam allowance is not necessary. Trace template onto the right side of the fabric with label facing up. Cut around shape on the traced line.

Piecing

Hand-Piecing Basics. When hand-piecing it is easier to begin with templates which do not include the 1/4" seam allowance. Place the template on the wrong side of the fabric, lining up the marked grain line with lengthwise or crosswise fabric grain. If the piece does not have to be reversed, place with labeled side up. Trace around shape; move, leaving 1/2" between the shapes, and mark again.

When you have marked the appropriate number of pieces, cut out pieces, leaving 1/4" beyond marked line all around each piece.

To piece, refer to assembly drawings to piece units and blocks, if provided. To join two units, place the patches with right sides together. Stick a pin in at the beginning of the seam through both fabric patches,

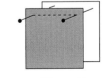

Figure 5
Stick a pin through fabrics to match the beginning of the seam.

matching the beginning points (Figure 5); for hand-piecing, the seam begins on the traced line, not at the edge of the fabric (see Figure 6).

Figure 6
Begin hand-piecing at seam, not at the edge of the fabric. Continue stitching along seam line.

Thread a sharp needle; knot one strand of the thread at the end. Remove the pin and insert the needle in the hole; make a short stitch and then a backstitch right over the first stitch.

Continue making short stitches with several stitches on the needle at one time. As you stitch, check the back piece often to assure accurate stitching on the seam line. Take a stitch at the end of the seam; back-stitch and knot at the same time as shown in Figure 7.

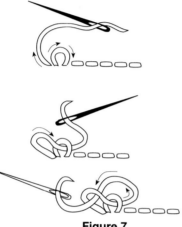

Figure 7
Make a loop in a backstitch to make a knot.

Seams on hand-pieced fabric patches may be finger-pressed toward the darker fabric.

To sew units together, pin fabric patches together, matching seams. Sew as above except where seams meet; at these intersections, backstitch, go through seam to next piece and backstitch again to secure seam joint.

Not all pieced blocks can be stitched with straight seams or in rows. Some patterns require set-in pieces. To begin a set-in seam on a star pattern, pin one side of the square to the proper side of the star point with right sides together, matching corners. Start stitching at the seam line on the outside point; stitch on the marked seam line to the end of the seam line at the center referring to Figure 8.

Bring around the adjacent side and pin to the next star point, matching seams. Continue the stitching line from the adjacent seam through corners

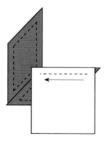

Figure 8
To set a square into a diamond point, match seams and stitch from outside edge to center.

and to the outside edge of the square as shown in Figure 9.

Machine-Piecing.
If making templates, include the 1/4" seam allowance on the template for machine-piecing. Place template on the wrong side of the fabric as for hand-piecing except butt pieces against one another when tracing.

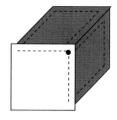

Figure 9
Continue stitching the adjacent side of the square to the next diamond shape in 1 seam from center to outside as shown.

Set machine on 2.5 or 12–15 stitches per inch. Join pieces as for hand-piecing for set-in seams; but for other straight seams, begin and end sewing at the end of the fabric patch sewn as shown in Figure 10. No backstitching is necessary when machine-stitching.

Figure 10
Begin machine-piecing at the end of the piece, not at the end of the seam.

Join units as for hand-piecing referring to the piecing diagrams where needed. Chain piecing (Figure 11—sewing several like units before sewing other units) saves time by eliminating beginning and ending stitches.

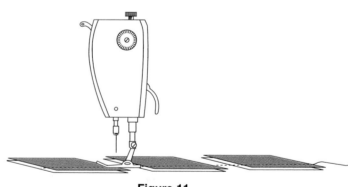

Figure 11
Units may be chain-pieced to save time.

When joining machine-pieced units, match seams against each other with seam allowances pressed in opposite directions to reduce bulk and make perfect matching of seams possible (Figure 12).

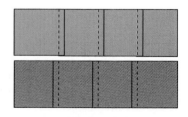

Figure 12
Sew machine-pieced units with seams pressed in opposite directions.

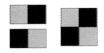

Cutting

Quick-Cutting. Quick-cutting and piecing strips are recommended for making many of the projects in this book. Templates are completely eliminated; instead, a rotary cutter, plastic ruler and mat are used to cut fabric pieces.

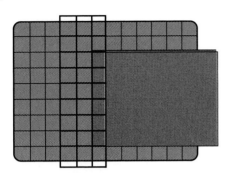

Figure 13
Fold fabric and straighten as shown.

When rotary-cutting strips, straighten raw edges of fabric by folding fabric in fourths across the width as shown in Figure 13. Press down flat; place ruler on fabric square with edge of fabric and make one cut from the folded edge to the outside edge. If strips are not straightened, a wavy strip will result as shown in Figure 14.

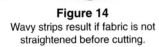

Figure 14
Wavy strips result if fabric is not straightened before cutting.

Always cut away from your body, holding the ruler firmly with the non-cutting hand. Keep fingers away from the edge of the ruler as it is easy for the rotary cutter to slip and jump over the edge of the ruler if cutting is not properly done.

For many strip-pieced blocks two strips are stitched together as shown in Figure 15. The strips are stitched, pressed and cut into segments as shown in Figure 16.

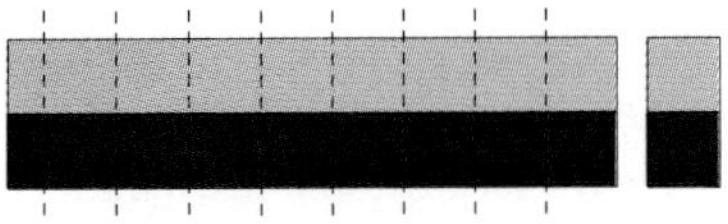

Figure 15
Join 2 strips as shown.

The cut segments are arranged as shown in Figure 17 and stitched to complete, in this example, one Four-

Figure 16
Cut segments from the stitched strip set.

Patch block. Although the block shown is very simple, the same methods may be used for more complicated patterns.

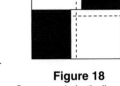

Figure 17
Arrange cut segments to make a Four-Patch block.

The direction to press seams on strip sets is important for accurate piecing later. The normal rule for pressing is to press seams toward the darker fabric to keep the colors from showing through on lighter colors later. For joining segments from strip sets, this rule doesn't always apply.

It is best if seams on adjacent rows are pressed in opposite directions. When aligning segments to stitch rows together, if pressed properly, seam joints will have a seam going in both directions as shown in Figure 18.

Figure 18
Seams go in both directions at seam joints.

If a square is required for the pattern, it can be subcut from a strip as shown in Figure 19.

Figure 19
If cutting squares, cut proper-width strip into same-width segments. Here, a 2" strip is cut into 2" segments to create 2" squares. These squares finish at 1 1/2" when sewn.

If you need right triangles with the straight grain on the short sides, you can use the same method, but you need to figure out how wide to cut the strip. Measure the finished size of one short side of the triangle. Add 7/8" to this size for seam allowance. Cut fabric strips this width; cut the strips into the same increment to create squares. Cut the squares on the diagonal to produce triangles. For example, if you need a triangle with a 2" finished height, cut the strips 2 7/8" by the width of the fabric. Cut the strips into 2 7/8" squares. Cut each square on the diagonal to produce the correct-size triangle with the grain on the short sides (Figure 20).

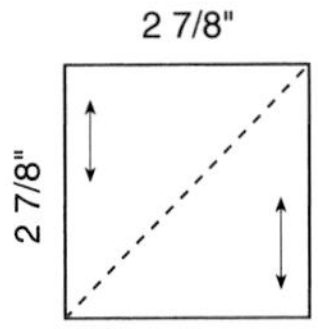

Figure 20
Cut 2" (finished size) triangles from 2 7/8" squares as shown.

Triangles sewn together to make squares are called

half-square triangles or triangle/squares. When joined, the triangle/square unit has the straight of grain on all outside edges of the block.

Another method of making triangle/squares is shown in Figure 21. Layer two squares with right sides

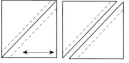

Figure 21
Mark a diagonal line on the square; stitch 1/4" on each side of the line. Cut on line to reveal stitched triangle/squares.

together; draw a diagonal line through the center. Stitch 1/4" on both sides of the line. Cut apart on the drawn line to reveal two stitched triangle/squares.

If you need triangles with the straight of grain on the diagonal, such as for fill-in triangles on the outside edges of a diagonal-set quilt, the procedure is a bit different.

To make these triangles, a square is cut on both diagonals; thus, the straight of grain is on the longest or diagonal side (Figure 22). To figure out the size to cut the square, add 1 1/4" to the needed finished size of the longest

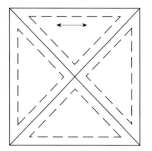

Figure 22
Add 1 1/4" to the finished size of the longest side of the triangle needed and cut on both diagonals to make a quarter-square triangle.

side of the triangle. For example, if you need a triangle with a 12" finished diagonal, cut a 13 1/4" square.

If templates are given, use their measurements to cut fabric strips to correspond with that measurement. The template may be used on the strip to cut pieces quickly. Strip cutting works best for squares, triangles, rectangles and diamonds. Odd-shaped templates are difficult to cut in multiple layers using a rotary cutter.

Foundation Piecing

Foundation Piecing. Paper or fabric foundation pieces are used to make very accurate blocks, provide stability for weak fabrics, and add body and weight to the finished quilt.

Temporary foundation materials include paper, tracing paper, freezer paper and removable interfacing. Permanent foundations include utility fabrics, non-woven interfacing, flannel, fleece and batting.

Methods of marking foundations include basting

lines, pencils or pens, needlepunching, tracing wheel, hot-iron transfers, copy machine, premarked, stamps or stencils.

There are two methods of foundation piecing—under-piecing and top-piecing. When under-piecing, the pattern is reversed when tracing. We have not included any patterns for top-piecing. *Note: All patterns for which we recommend paper piecing are already reversed in full-size drawings given.*

To under-piece, place a scrap of fabric larger than the lined space on the unlined side of the paper in the No. 1 position. Place piece 2 right sides together with piece 1; pin on seam line, and fold back to check that the piece will cover space 2 before stitching.

Stitch along line on the lined side of the paper—fabric will not be visible. Sew several stitches beyond the beginning and ending of the line. Backstitching is not required as another fabric seam will cover this seam.

Remove pin; finger-press piece 2 flat. Continue adding all pieces in numerical order in the same manner until all pieces are stitched to paper. Trim excess to outside line (1/4" larger all around than finished size of the block).

Tracing paper can be used as a temporary foundation. It is removed when blocks are complete and stitched together. To paper-piece, copy patterns using a copy machine or trace each block individually. Measure the finished paper foundations to insure accuracy in copying.

Appliqué

Appliqué is the process of applying one piece of fabric on top of another for decorative or functional purposes.

Making Templates. Most appliqué designs given here are shown as full-size drawings for the completed designs. The drawings show dotted lines to indicate where one piece overlaps another. Other marks indicate placement of embroidery stitches for decorative purposes such as eyes, lips, flowers, etc.

For hand appliqué, trace each template onto the right side of the fabric with template right side up. Cut around shape, adding a 1/8"–1/4" seam allowance.

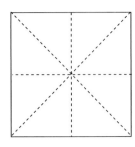

Figure 23
Fold background to mark centers as shown.

Before the actual appliqué process begins, cut the background block and prepare it for stitching. Most appliqué designs are centered on the block. To find the center of the background square, fold it in half and in half again; crease with your fingers. Now unfold and fold diagonally and crease; repeat for other corners referring to Figure 23. Center-line creases help position the design. If centering the appliqué design is important, an X has been placed on each drawing to mark the center of the design. Match the X with the creased center of the background block when placing pieces.

If you have a full-size drawing of the design, as is given with most appliqué designs in this book, it might help you to draw on the background block to help with placement. Transfer the design to a large piece of tracing paper. Place the paper on top of the design; use masking tape to hold in place. Trace design onto paper.

If you don't have a light box, tape the pattern on a window; center the background block on top and tape in place. Trace the design onto the background block with a water-erasable marker or chalk pencil. This drawing will mark exactly where the fabric pieces should be placed on the background block.

Hand Appliqué. Traditional hand appliqué uses a template made from the desired finished shape without seam allowance added.

After fabric is prepared, trace the desired shape onto the right side of the fabric with a water-erasable marker, light lead or chalk pencil. Leave at least 1/2" between design motifs when tracing to allow for the seam allowance when cutting out the shapes.

When the desired number of shapes needed has been drawn on the fabric pieces, cut out shapes leaving 1/8"–1/4" all around drawn line for turning under.

Turn the shape's edges over on the drawn or stitched line. When turning the edges under, make sharp corners

sharp and smooth edges smooth. The fabric patch should retain the shape of the template used to cut it.

When turning in concave curves, clip to seams and baste the seam allowance over as shown in Figure 24.

Figure 24
Concave curves should be clipped before turning as shown.

During the actual appliqué process, you may be layering one shape on top of another. Where two fabrics overlap, the underneath piece does not have to be turned under or stitched down.

If possible, trim away the underneath fabric when the block is finished by carefully cutting away the background from underneath and then cutting away unnecessary layers to reduce bulk and avoid shadows from darker fabrics showing through on light fabrics.

For hand appliqué, position the fabric shapes on the background block and pin or baste them in place. Using a blind stitch or appliqué stitch, sew pieces in place with matching thread and small stitches. Start with background pieces first and work up to foreground pieces. Appliqué the pieces in place on the background in numerical order, if given, layering as necessary.

Machine Appliqué. There are several products available to help make the machine-appliqué process easier and faster.

Fusible transfer web is a commercial product similar to iron-on interfacings except it has two sticky sides. It is used to adhere appliqué shapes to the background with heat. Paper is adhered to one side of the web.

To use, dry-iron the sticky side of the fusible product onto the wrong side of the chosen fabric. Draw desired shapes onto the paper and cut them out. Peel off the paper and dry-iron the shapes in place on the background fabric. The shape will stay in place while you stitch around it. This process adds a little bulk or stiffness to the appliquéd shape and makes hand quilting through the layers difficult.

For successful machine appliqué a tear-off stabilizer is recommended. This product is placed under the background fabric while machine appliqué is being done. It is torn away when the work is finished. This kind of stabilizer keeps the background fabric from pulling during the machine-appliqué process.

During the actual machine-appliqué process, you will be layering one shape on top of another. Where two fabrics overlap, the underneath piece does not have to be turned under or stitched down.

Thread the top of the machine with thread to match the fabric patches or with threads that coordinate or contrast with fabrics. Rayon thread is a good choice when a sheen is desired on the finished appliqué stitches. Do not use rayon thread in the bobbin; use all-purpose thread.

Set your machine to make a zigzag stitch and practice on scraps of similar weight to check the tension. If you can see the bobbin thread on the top of the appliqué, adjust your machine to make a balanced stitch. Different-width stitches are available; choose one that will not overpower the appliqué shapes. In some cases these appliqué stitches will be used as decorative stitches as well and you may want the thread to show.

If using a stabilizer, place this under the background fabric and pin or fuse in place. Place shapes as for

Tips & Techniques

Before machine-piecing fabric patches together, test your sewing machine for positioning an accurate 1/4" seam allowance. There are several tools to help guarantee this. Some machine needles may be moved to allow the presser-foot edge to be a 1/4" guide.

A special foot may be purchased for your machine that will guarantee an accurate 1/4" seam. A piece of masking tape can be placed on the throat plate of your sewing machine to mark the 1/4" seam. A plastic stick-on ruler may be used instead of tape with the same results.

hand-appliqué and stitch all around shapes by machine.

When all machine work is complete, remove stabilizer from the back referring to the manufacturer's instructions.

Putting It All Together

Many steps are required to prepare a quilt top for quilting, including setting the blocks together, adding borders, choosing and marking quilting designs, layering the top, batting and backing for quilting, quilting or tying the layers and finishing the edges of the quilt.

As you begin the process of finishing your quilt top, strive for a neat, flat quilt with square sides and corners, not for perfection—that will come with time and practice.

Finishing the Top

Settings. Most quilts are made by sewing individual blocks together in rows which, when joined, create a design. There are several other methods used to join blocks. Sometimes the setting choice is determined by the block's design. For example, a house block should be placed upright on a quilt, not sideways or upside down.

Plain blocks can be alternated with pieced or appliquéd blocks in a straight set. Making a quilt using plain blocks saves time; half the number of pieced or appliquéd blocks are needed to make the same-size quilt as shown in Figure 1.

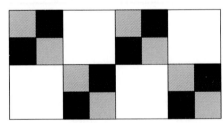

Figure 1
Alternate plain blocks with pieced blocks to save time.

Adding Borders. Borders are an integral part of the quilt and should complement the colors and designs used in the quilt center. Borders frame a quilt just like a mat and frame do a picture.

If fabric strips are added for borders, they may be mitered or butted at the corners as shown in Figures 2 and 3.

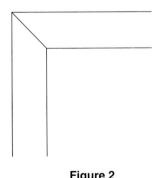

Figure 2
Mitered corners look like this.

To determine the size for butted-border strips, measure across the center of the completed quilt top from one side raw edge to the other side raw edge. This measurement will include a 1/4" seam allowance. Cut two border strips that length by the chosen width of the border. Sew these strips to the top and bottom of the pieced center referring to Figure 4. Press the seam allowance toward the border strips.

Measure across the completed quilt top at the center, from top raw edge to bottom raw edge, including the two border strips already added. Cut two border strips that length by the chosen width of the border. Sew a strip to each of the two remaining sides as shown in Figure 4. Press the seams toward the border strips.

To make mitered corners, measure the quilt as before. To this add twice the width of the border and 1/2" for seam allowances to determine the length of the strips. Repeat for opposite sides. Center and sew on each strip, stopping

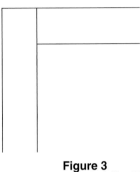

Figure 3
Butted corners look like this.

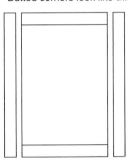

Figure 4
Sew border strips to opposite sides; sew remaining 2 strips to remaining sides to make butted corners.

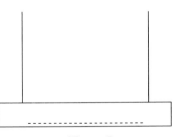

Figure 5
For mitered corner, stitch strip, stopping 1/4" from corner seam.

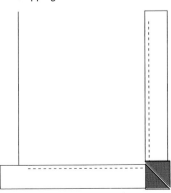

Figure 6
Fold and press corner to make a 45-degree angle.

stitching 1/4" from corner, leaving the remainder of the strip dangling.

Press corners at a 45-degree angle to form a crease. Stitch from the inside quilt corner to the outside on the creased line. Trim excess away after stitching and press mitered seams open (Figures 5–7).

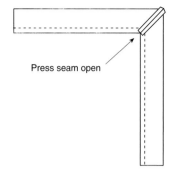

Figure 7
Trim away excess from underneath when stitching is complete. Press seams open.

Carefully press the entire quilt top. Avoid pulling and stretching while pressing, which would distort shapes.

Getting Ready to Quilt

Choosing a Quilting Design. If you choose to hand- or machine-quilt your finished top, you will need to choose a design for quilting.

There are several types of quilting designs, some of which may not have to be marked. The easiest of the unmarked designs is in-the-ditch quilting. Here the quilting stitches are placed in the valley created by the seams joining two pieces together or next to the edge of an appliqué design. There is no need to mark a top for in-the-ditch quilting. Machine quilters choose this option because the stitches are not as obvious on the finished quilt (Figure 8).

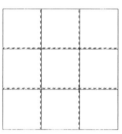

Figure 8
In-the-ditch quilting is done in the seam that joins 2 pieces.

Outline-quilting 1/4" or more away from seams or appliqué shapes is another no-mark alternative (Figure 9) which prevents having to sew through the layers made by seams, thus making stitching easier.

If you are not comfortable eyeballing the 1/4" (or other distance), masking tape is available in different widths and is helpful to place on straight-edge designs to mark the quilting line. If using masking tape, place the tape right up against the seam and quilt close to the other edge.

Figure 9
Outline-quilting 1/4" away from seam is a popular choice for quilting.

Meander or free-motion quilting by machine fills in open spaces and doesn't require marking. It is fun and easy to stitch as shown in Figure 10.

Marking the Top for Quilting or Tying. If you choose a fancy or all-over design for quilting, you will need to transfer the design to your quilt top before layering with the backing and batting. You may use a sharp medium-lead or silver pencil on light background fabrics. Test the pencil marks to guarantee that they will wash out of your quilt top when quilting is complete; or be sure your quilting stitches cover the pencil marks. Mechanical pencils with very fine points may be used successfully to mark quilts.

Figure 10
Machine meander quilting fills in large spaces.

Manufactured quilt-design templates are available in many designs and sizes and are cut out of a durable plastic template material which is easy to use.

To make a permanent quilt-design template, choose a template material on which to transfer the design. See-through plastic is the best as it will let you place the design while allowing you to see where it is in relation to your quilt design without moving it. Place the design on the quilt top where you want it and trace around it with your marking tool. Pick up the quilting template and place again; repeat marking.

No matter what marking method you use, remember—the marked lines should never show on the finished quilt. When the top is marked, it is ready for layering.

Preparing the Quilt Backing. The quilt backing is a very important feature of your quilt. In most cases, the materials list for each quilt in this book gives the size requirements for the backing, not the yardage needed. Exceptions to this are when the backing fabric is also used on the quilt top and yardage is given for that fabric.

A backing is generally cut at least 4" larger than the quilt top or 2" larger on all sides. For a 64" x 78" finished quilt, the backing would need to be at least 68" x 82".

To avoid having the seam across the center of the quilt backing, cut or tear

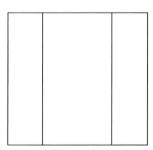

Figure 11
Center 1 backing piece with a piece on each side.

one of the right-length pieces in half and sew half to each side of the second piece as shown in Figure 11.

Quilts that need backing more than 88" wide may be pieced in horizontal pieces as shown in Figure 12.

Layering the Quilt Sandwich. Layering the quilt top with the batting and backing is time-consuming. Open the batting several days before you need it and place

Figure 12
Horizontal seams may be used on backing pieces.

over a bed or flat on the floor to help flatten the creases caused from its being folded up in the bag for so long.

Iron the backing piece, folding in half both vertically and horizontally and pressing to mark centers.

If you will not be quilting on a frame, place the backing right side down on a clean floor or table. Start in the center and push any wrinkles or bunches flat. Use masking tape to tape the edges to the floor or large clips to hold the backing to the edges of the table. The backing should be taut.

Place the batting on top of the backing, matching centers using fold lines as guides; flatten out any wrinkles. Trim the batting to the same size as the backing.

Fold the quilt top in half lengthwise and place on top of the batting, wrong side against the batting, matching centers. Unfold quilt and, working from the center to the outside edges, smooth out any wrinkles or lumps.

To hold the quilt layers together for quilting, baste by hand or use safety pins. If basting by hand, thread a long thin needle with a long piece of unknotted white or off-white thread. Starting in the center and leaving a long tail, make 4"–6" stitches toward the outside edge of the quilt top, smoothing as you baste. Start at the center again and work toward the outside as shown in Figure 13.

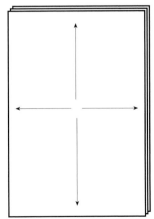

Figure 13
Baste from the center to the outside edges.

If quilting by machine, you may prefer to use safety pins for holding your quilt sandwich together. Start in the center of the quilt and pin to the outside, leaving pins open until all are placed. When you are satisfied that all layers are smooth, close the pins.

Quilting

Hand Quilting. Hand quilting is the process of placing stitches through the quilt top, batting and backing to hold them together. While it is a functional process, it also adds beauty and loft to the finished quilt.

To begin, thread a sharp between needle with an 18" piece of quilting thread. Tie a small knot in the end of the thread. Position the needle about 1/2" to 1" away from the starting point on quilt top. Sink the needle through the top into the batting layer but not through the backing. Pull

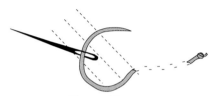

Figure 14
Start the needle through the top layer of fabric 1/2"–1" away from quilting line with knot on top of fabric.

Tips & Techniques

Knots should not show on the quilt top or back. Learn to sink the knot into the batting at the beginning and ending of the quilting thread for successful stitches.

When you have nearly run out of thread, wind the thread around the needle several times to make a small knot and pull it close to the fabric. Insert the needle into the fabric on the quilting line and come out with the needle 1/2" to 1" away, pulling the knot into the fabric layers the same as when you started. Pull and cut thread close to fabric. The end should disappear inside after cutting. Some quilters prefer to take a backstitch with a loop through it for a knot to end.

Making 12–18 stitches per inch is a nice goal, but a more realistic goal is seven to nine stitches per inch. If you cannot accomplish this right away, strive for even stitches—all the same size—that look as good on the back as on the front.

You will perfect your quilting stitches as you gain experience, your stitches will get better with each project and your style will be uniquely your own.

the needle up at the starting point of the quilting design. Pull the needle and thread until the knot sinks through the top into the batting (Figure 14).

Some stitchers like to take a backstitch at the beginning while others prefer to begin the first stitch here. Take small, even running stitches along the marked quilting line (Figure 15). Keep one hand positioned underneath to feel the needle go all the way through to the backing.

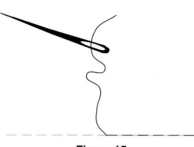

Figure 15
Make small, even running stitches on marked quilting line.

Machine Quilting. Successful machine quilting requires practice and a good relationship with your sewing machine.

Prepare the quilt for machine quilting in the same way as for hand quilting. Use safety pins to hold the layers together instead of basting with thread.

Presser-foot quilting is best used for straight-line quilting because the presser bar lever does not need to be continually lifted.

Set the machine on a longer stitch length (3 or eight to 10 stitches to the inch). Too tight a stitch causes puckering and fabric tucks, either on the quilt top or backing. An even-feed or walking foot helps to eliminate the tucks and puckering by feeding the upper and lower layers through the machine evenly. Before you begin, loosen the amount of pressure on the presser foot.

Special machine-quilting needles work best to penetrate the three layers in your quilt.

Decide on a design. Quilting in the ditch is not quite as visible, but if you quilt with the feed dogs engaged, it means turning the quilt frequently. It is not easy to fit a rolled-up quilt through the small opening on the sewing machine head.

Meander quilting is the easiest way to machine-quilt—and it is fun. Meander quilting is done using an appliqué or darning foot with the feed dogs dropped. It is sort of like scribbling. Simply move the quilt top around under the foot and make stitches in a random pattern to fill the space. The same method may be used to outline a quilt design. The trick is the same as in

---

Tips & Techniques

Use a thimble to prevent sore fingers when hand quilting. The finger that is under the quilt to feel the needle as it passes through the backing is the one that is most apt to get sore from the pin pricks. Some quilters purchase leather thimbles for this finger while others try home remedies. One simple aid is masking tape wrapped around the finger. With the tape you will still be able to feel the needle, but it will not prick your skin. Over time calluses build up and these fingers get toughened up, but with every vacation from quilting, they will become soft and the process begins again.

When you feel your shoulder muscles tensing up, take a rest.

---

hand-quilting; you are striving for stitches of uniform size. Your hands are in complete control of the design.

If machine-quilting is of interest to you, there are several very good books available at quilt shops that will help you become a successful machine quilter.

Tied Quilts, or Comforters. Would you rather tie your quilt layers together than quilt them? Tied quilts are often referred to as comforters. The advantage of tying is that it takes so much less time and the required skills can be learned quickly.

If a top will be tied, choose a thick, bonded batting—one that will not separate during washing. For tying, use pearl cotton, embroidery floss, or strong yarn in colors that match or coordinate with the fabrics in your quilt top.

Decide on a pattern for tying. Many quilts are tied at the corners and centers of the blocks and at sashing joints. Try to tie every 4"–6". Special designs can be used for tying, but most quilts are tied in conventional ways. Begin tying in the center and work to the outside edges.

To make the tie, thread a large needle with a long thread (yarn, floss or crochet cotton); do not knot. Push the needle through the quilt top to the back, leaving a 3"–4" length on top. Move the needle to the next position without cutting thread. Take another stitch through the layers; repeat until thread is almost used up.

Cut thread between stitches, leaving an equal amount of thread on each stitch. Tie a knot with the two thread ends. Tie again to make a square knot referring to Figure

16. Trim thread ends to desired length.

Finishing the Edges

Figure 16
Make a square knot as shown.

After your quilt is tied or quilted, the edges need to be finished. Decide how you want the edges of your quilt finished before layering the backing and batting with the quilt top.

Without Binding—Self-Finish. There is one way to eliminate adding an edge finish. This is done before quilting. Place the batting on a flat surface. Place the pieced top right side up on the batting. Place the backing right sides together with the pieced top. Pin and/or baste the layers together to hold flat referring to page 171.

Begin stitching in the center of one side using a 1/4" seam allowance, reversing at the beginning and end of the seam. Continue stitching all around and back to the beginning side. Leave a 12" or larger opening. Clip corners to reduce excess. Turn right side out through the opening. Slipstitch the opening closed by hand. The quilt may now be quilted by hand or machine.

The disadvantage to this method is that once the edges are sewn in, any creases or wrinkles that might form during the quilting process cannot be flattened out. Tying is the preferred method for finishing a quilt constructed using this method.

Bringing the backing fabric to the front is another way to finish the quilt's edge without binding. To accomplish this, complete the quilt as for hand or machine quilting. Trim the batting *only* even with the front. Trim the backing 1" larger than the completed top all around.

Turn the backing edge in 1/2" and then turn over to the front along edge of batting. The folded edge may be machine-stitched close to the edge through all layers, or blind-stitched in place to finish.

The front may be turned to the back. If using this method, a wider front border is needed. The backing and batting are trimmed 1" smaller than the top and the top edge is turned under 1/2" and then turned to the back and stitched in place.

One more method of self-finish may be used. The top and backing may be stitched together by hand at the edge. To accomplish this, all quilting must be stopped 1/2" from the quilt-top edge. The top and backing of

the quilt are trimmed even and the batting is trimmed to 1/4"–1/2" smaller. The edges of the top and backing are turned in 1/4"–1/2" and blind-stitched together at the very edge.

These methods do not require the use of extra fabric and save time in preparation of binding strips; they are not as durable as an added binding.

Binding. The technique of adding extra fabric at the edges of the quilt is called binding. The binding encloses the edges and adds an extra layer of fabric for durability.

To prepare the quilt for the addition of the binding, trim the batting and backing layers flush with the top of the quilt using a rotary cutter and ruler or shears. Using a walking-foot attachment (sometimes called an even-feed foot attachment), machine-baste the three layers together all around approximately 1/8" from the cut edge.

The list of materials given with each quilt in this book often includes a number of yards of self-made or purchased binding. Bias binding may be purchased in packages and in many colors. The advantage to self-made binding is that you can use fabrics from your quilt to coordinate colors.

Double-fold, straight-grain binding and double-fold, bias-grain binding are two of the most commonly used types of binding.

Double-fold, straight-grain binding is used on smaller projects with right-angle corners. Double-fold, bias-grain binding is best suited for bed-size quilts or quilts with rounded corners.

To make double-fold, straight-grain binding, cut 2"-wide strips of fabric across the width or down the length of the fabric totaling the perimeter of the quilt plus 10". The strips are joined as shown in Figure 17 and pressed in half wrong sides together along the length using an iron on a cotton setting with no steam.

Figure 17
Join binding strips in a diagonal seam to eliminate bulk as shown.

Lining up the raw edges, place the binding on the top of the quilt and begin sewing (again using the walking foot) approximately 6" from the beginning of the binding strip. Stop sewing 1/4" from the first corner, leave the needle in the quilt, turn and sew diagonally to the corner as shown in Figure 18.

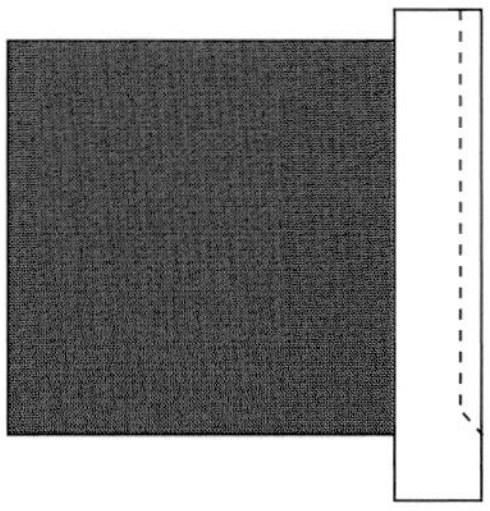

Fold the binding at a 45-degree angle up and away from the quilt as shown in Figure 19 and back down flush with the raw edges. Starting at the top raw edge of the quilt, begin sewing the next side as shown in Figure 20. Repeat at the next three corners.

Figure 18
Sew to within 1/4" of corner; leave needle in quilt, turn and stitch diagonally off the corner of the quilt.

As you approach the beginning of the binding strip, stop stitching and over-lap the binding 1/2" from the edge; trim. Join the two ends with a 1/4" seam allowance and press the seam open. Reposition the joined binding along the edge of the quilt and resume stitching to the beginning.

To finish, bring the folded edge of the binding over the raw edges and blind-stitch the binding in place over the machine-stitching line on the back-side. Hand-miter the corners on the back as shown in Figure 21.

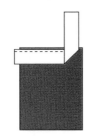

Figure 19
Fold binding at a 45-degree angle up and away from quilt as shown.

If you are making a quilt to be used on a bed, you will want to use double-fold, bias-grain bindings because the many threads that cross each other along the fold at the edge of the quilt make it a more durable binding.

Cut 2"-wide bias strips from a large square of fabric. Join the strips as illustrated in Figure 17 and press the seams open. Fold the beginning end of the bias strip 1/4" from the raw edge and press. Fold the joined strips in half along the long side, wrong sides together, and press with no steam (Figure 22).

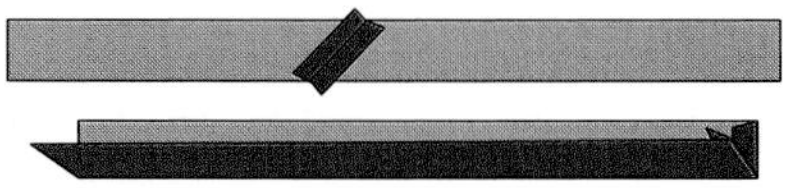

Figure 20
Fold the binding strips back down, flush with the raw edge, and begin sewing.

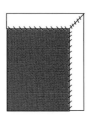

Figure 21
Miter and stitch the corners as shown.

Follow the same procedures as previously described for preparing the quilt top and sewing the binding to the

Figure 22
Fold end in and press strip in half.

quilt top. Treat the corners just as you treated them with straight-grain binding.

Since you are using bias-grain binding, you do have the option to just eliminate the corners if this option doesn't interfere with the patchwork in the quilt. Round the corners off by placing one of your din-ner plates at the corner and rotary-cutting the gentle curve (Figure 23).

Figure 23
Round corners to eliminate square-corner finishes.

As you approach the beginning of the binding strip, stop stitching and lay the end across the beginning so it will slip inside the fold. Cut the end at a 45-degree angle so the raw edges

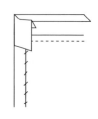

Figure 24
End the binding strips as shown.

are contained inside the beginning of the strip (Figure 24). Resume stitching to the beginning. Bring the fold to the back of the quilt and hand-stitch as previ-ously described.

Overlapped corners are not quite as easy as rounded ones, but a bit easier than mitering. To make overlapped corners, sew binding strips to opposite sides of the quilt top. Stitch edges down to finish. Trim ends even.

Sew a strip to each remaining side, leaving 1 1/2"–2" excess at each end. Turn quilt over and fold end in even with previous finished edge as shown in Figure 25.

Figure 25
Fold end of binding even with previous edge.

Fold binding in toward quilt and stitch down as before, enclosing the previous bound edge in the seam as shown in Figure 26. It may be necessary to trim the folded-down section to reduce bulk.

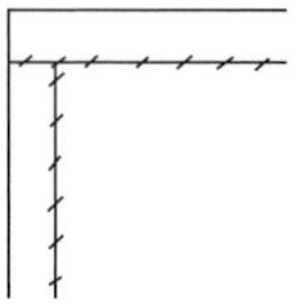

Figure 26
An overlapped corner is not quite as neat as a mitered corner.

Making Continuous Bias Binding

Instead of cutting individual bias strips and sewing them together, you may make continuous bias binding.

Cut a square 18" x 18" from chosen binding fabric. Cut the square once on the diagonal to make two triangles as shown in Figure 27. With right sides together, sew the two triangles together with a 1/4" seam allowance as shown in Figure 28; press seam open to reduce bulk.

Mark lines every 2 1/4" on the wrong side of the fabric as shown in Figure 29. Bring the short ends together, right sides together, offsetting one line as shown in Figure 30 to make a tube; stitch. This will seem awkward.

Begin cutting at point A as shown in Figure 31; continue cutting along marked line to make one continuous strip. Fold strip in half along length with wrong sides together; press. Sew to quilt edges as instructed previously for bias binding.

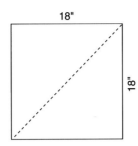

Figure 27
Cut 18" square on the diagonal.

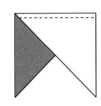

Figure 28
Sew the triangles together.

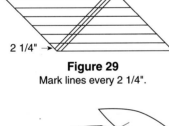

2 1/4"

Figure 29
Mark lines every 2 1/4".

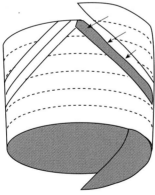

Figure 30
Sew short ends together,
offsetting lines to make a tube.

Final Touches

If your quilt will be hung on the wall, a hanging sleeve is required. Other options include purchased plastic rings or fabric tabs. The best choice is a fabric sleeve, which will evenly distribute the weight of the quilt across the top edge, rather than at selected spots where tabs or rings are stitched, keep the quilt hanging straight and not damage the batting.

To make a sleeve, measure across the top of the finished quilt. Cut an 8"-wide piece of muslin equal to that length—you may need to seam several muslin strips together to make the required length.

Fold in 1/4" on each end of the muslin strip and press. Fold again and stitch to hold. Fold the muslin strip lengthwise with right sides together. Sew along the long side to make a tube. Turn the tube right side out; press with seam at bottom or centered on the back.

Hand-stitch the tube along the top of the quilt and the bottom of the tube to the quilt back making sure the quilt lies flat. Stitches should not go through to the front of the quilt and don't need to be too close together as shown in Figure 32.

Slip a wooden dowel or long curtain rod through the sleeve to hang.

When the quilt is finally complete, it should be signed and dated. Use a permanent pen on the back of the quilt. Other methods include cross-stitching your name and date on the front or back or making a permanent label which may be stitched to the back.

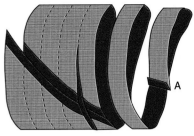

Figure 31
Cut along marked lines, starting at A.

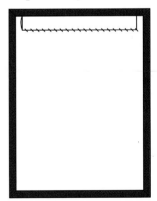

Figure 32
Sew a sleeve to the top
back of the quilt

Special Thanks

We would like to thank the talented quilt designers whose works are featured in this collection.

Kathy Brown
Patch Happy Jumper, 102

Michele Crawford
My Little Kitty, 36

Holly Daniels
Checkerboard Star Vest and Purse, 51
Zigzag Denim Exercise Mat and Duffle Bag, 108
Jumbles Lap Quilt and Pillow, 159

Lucy Fazely
Bright Triangles, 156

Sandra Hatch
Crazy-Patch Star, 16

Connie Kauffman
I Love the Blues, 68

Pearl Krush
Americana Shirt, Skirt and Tote, 98

Mary Jo Kurten
Pine Tree, 8

Sunflower Star, 21
Kitty Corner, 28

Kate Laucomer
Hearts in the Pines, 64

Janice Loewenthal
Home Sweet Home, 82

Patsy Moreland
Crazy-Patch and Plaid Christmas Stocking, 114

Karen Neary
Christmas Star Tie, 58
Snowed Under Tie, 60
Pick o' the Irish Tie, 61

Judith Sandstrom
Stripe Mosiac, 128
Scrappy Baby Quilt and Happy the Clown, 131
Secret Star Ensemble, 152

Marian Shenk
Rosy Red Apple Kitchen Set, 75
Denim Bandanna Picnic Trio, 105

Barb Sprunger
Delectable Mountains Variation, 12

Jeanne Stauffer
Multiple Irish Chain, 24

Charlyne Stewart
Crazy-Patch Jacket and Skirt, 44

Norma Storm
Sweetheart Wreath Table Runner and Coasters, 87

Ruth Swasey
Bowl of Roses Quilt and Pillow, 138
Stars & Stripes Quilt and Dresser Scarf, 143
Crosswinds Quilt and Valance, 147

Beth Wheeler
Memories Vest, 34
Baskets of Flowers Cardigan, 40
Autumn Glory Cardigan, 55
Ladybug Table Set, 92
Denim Doggie and
  Dorm-Room Throw, 120

Johanna Wilson
Quilt Bock Vest and Skirt, 46

Fabrics & Supplies

Page 36: My Little Kitty—Pellon WonderUnder fusible transfer web and Stitch-n-Tear tear-off stabilizer.

Page 58: Christmas Star Tie—Pellon Stitch-n-Tear tear-off fabric stabilizer and medium-weight fusible interfacing and YLI gold metallic thread.

Page 60: Snowed Under Tie—Pellon Stitch-n-Tear tear-off fabric stabilizer and medium-weight fusible interfacing and YLI orange, black and silver machine-embroidery thread.

Page 60: Snowed Under Tie—Pellon Stitch-n-Tear tear-off fabric stabilizer,

Wonder Under fusible transfer web and medium-weight fusible interfacing and YLI orange, black and silver machine embroidery-thread.

Page 82: Samples stitched by Sue Harvey.

Page 105: Denim Bandanna Picnic Trio—Simplicitiy pattern 7889 for apron and 8690 for mitt.

Page 118: Crazy-Patch and Plaid Stocking—Schmetz 120/705HJ size 90/14 sewing machine needle, Steam-A-Seam 2R from The Warm Co. and metallic threads from Sulky of America.

Page 120: Dorm-Room Throw—Fray Block from June Tailor used to prevent fraying.

Page 128: Stripe Mosaic—Hobbs Heirloom cotton batting and Fiskars rotary-cutting equipment.

Page 131: Scrappy Baby Quilt and Happy the Clown—Hobbs Heirloom cotton batting, Red Heart Classic 336 Warm Brown yarn and Fiskars rotary-cutting tools.

Page 156: Bright Triangles—Mr. B's Brights fabric collection from Benartex Inc., Mountain Mist quilt batting from The Stearns Technical Textiles Co., and machine quilting by Tyler's Machine Quilting Service.